THE DEVIL'S CONCUBINE

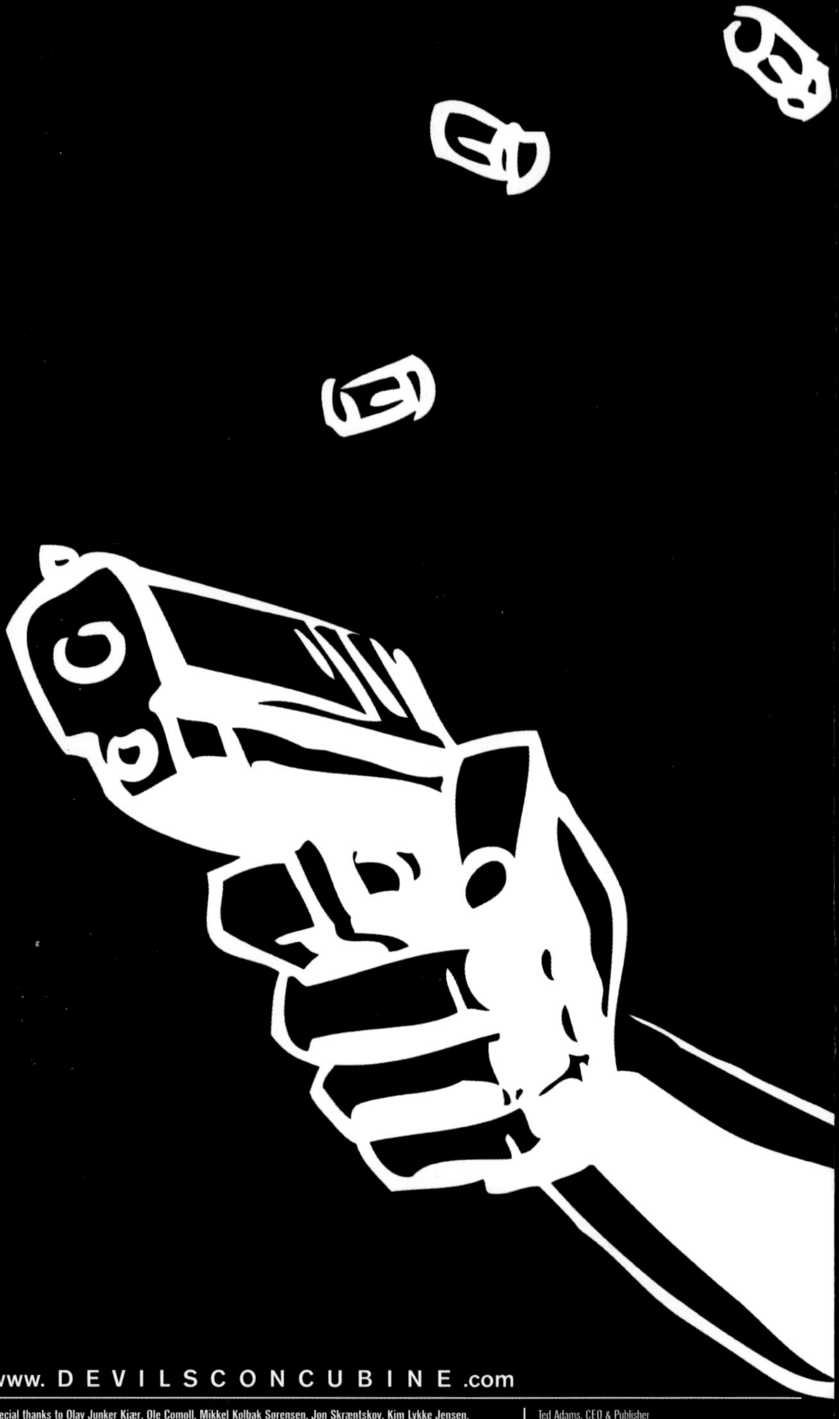

www. D E V I L S C O N C U B I N E .com

IDW

Special thanks to Olav Junker Kjær, Ole Comoll, Mikkel Kolbak Sørensen, Jon Skræntskov, Kim Lykke Jensen, Erling Lynder, Rune Christensen, Scott Dille, Alan Emmins, and Peter Snejbjerg for their invaluable assistance.

ISBN: 978-1-60010-948-5 14 13 12 11 1 2 3 4

www.IDWPUBLISHING.com

Originally published as BLODETS KONKUBINE in Denmark.

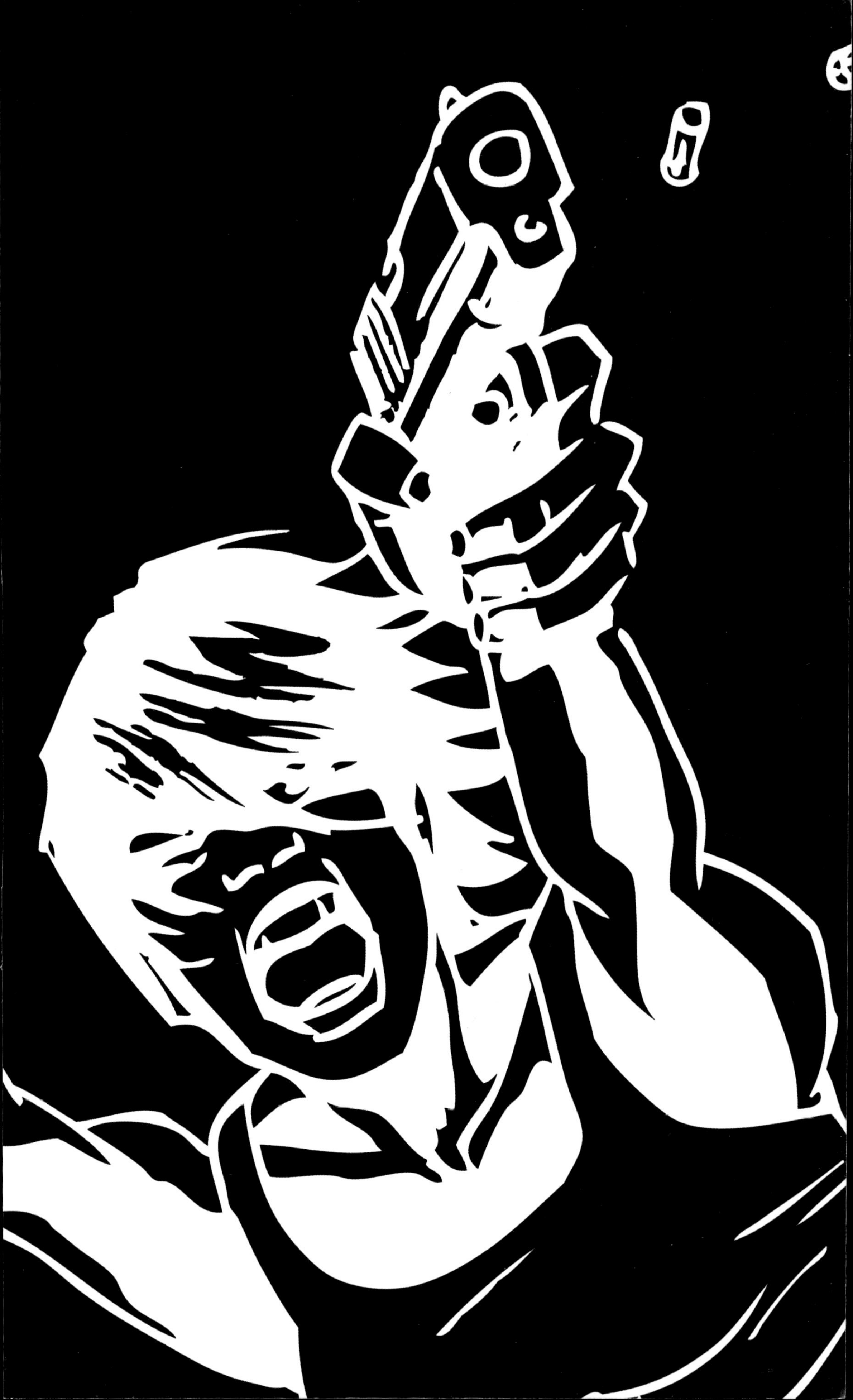

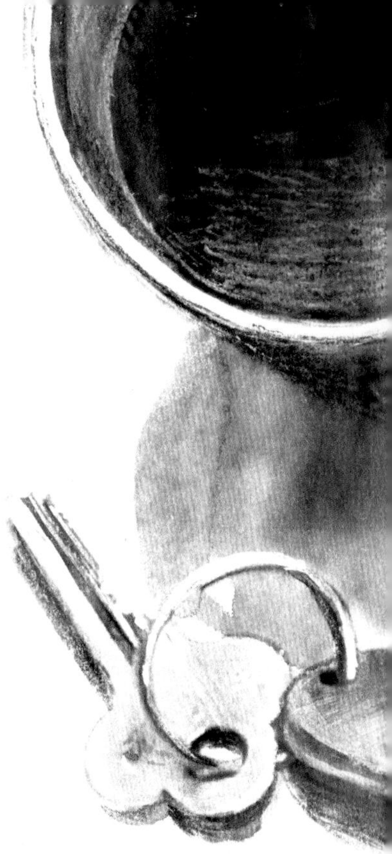

Created, written, drawn, and colored by

Palle Schmidt

Edits by

Denton J. Tipton

Design by

Shawn Lee

Cover by

Peter Snejbjerg

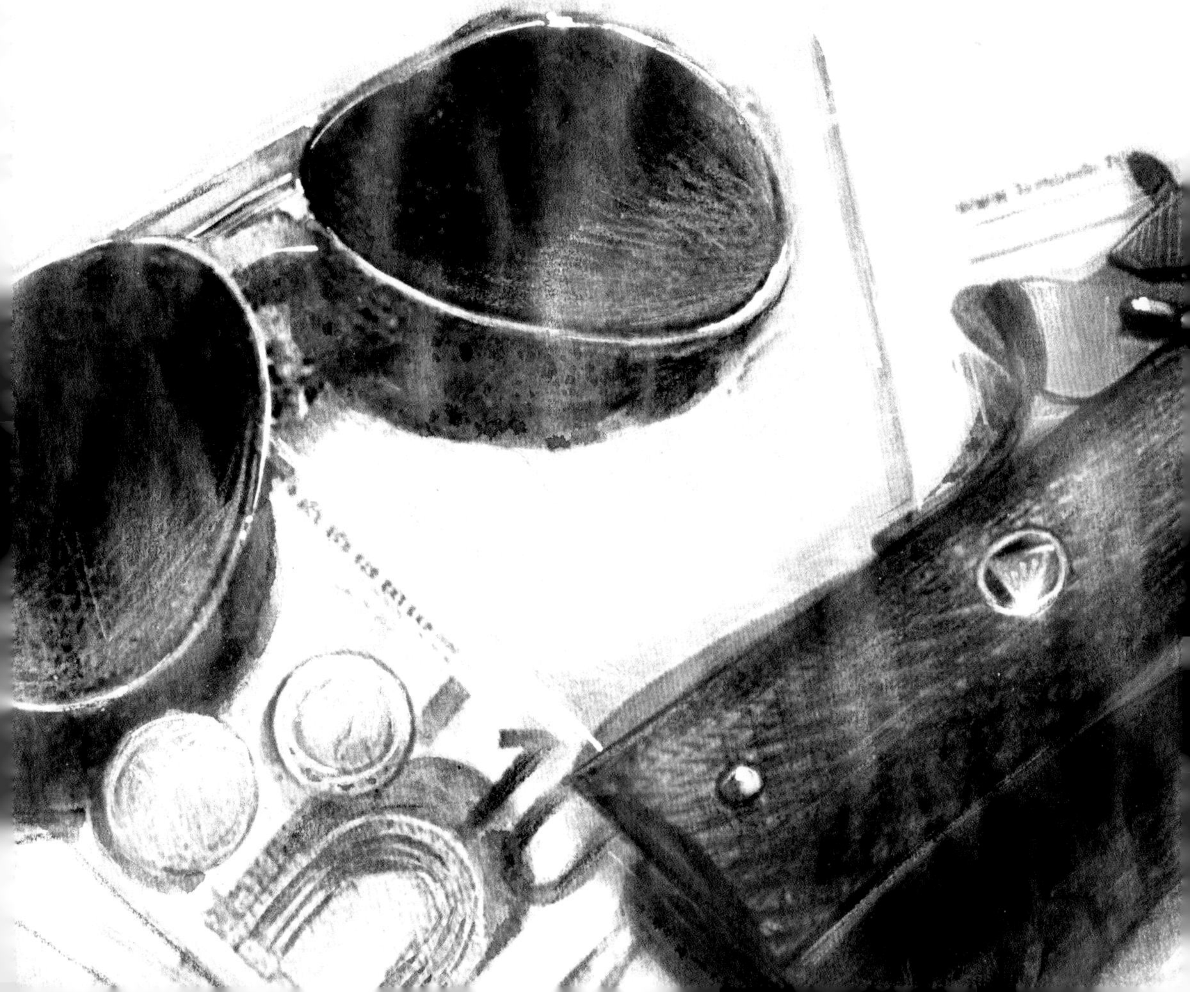

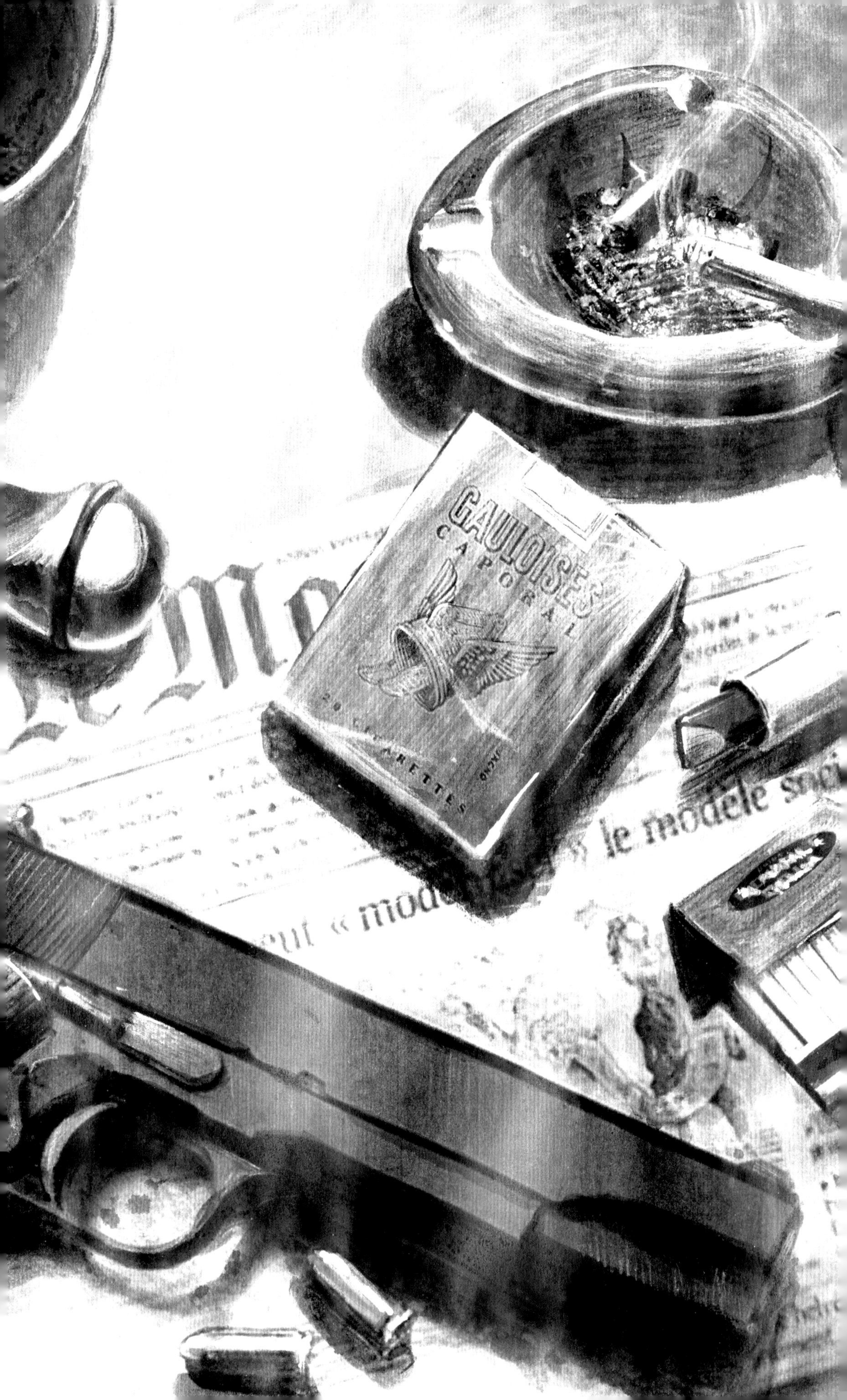
GAULOISES
CAPORAL

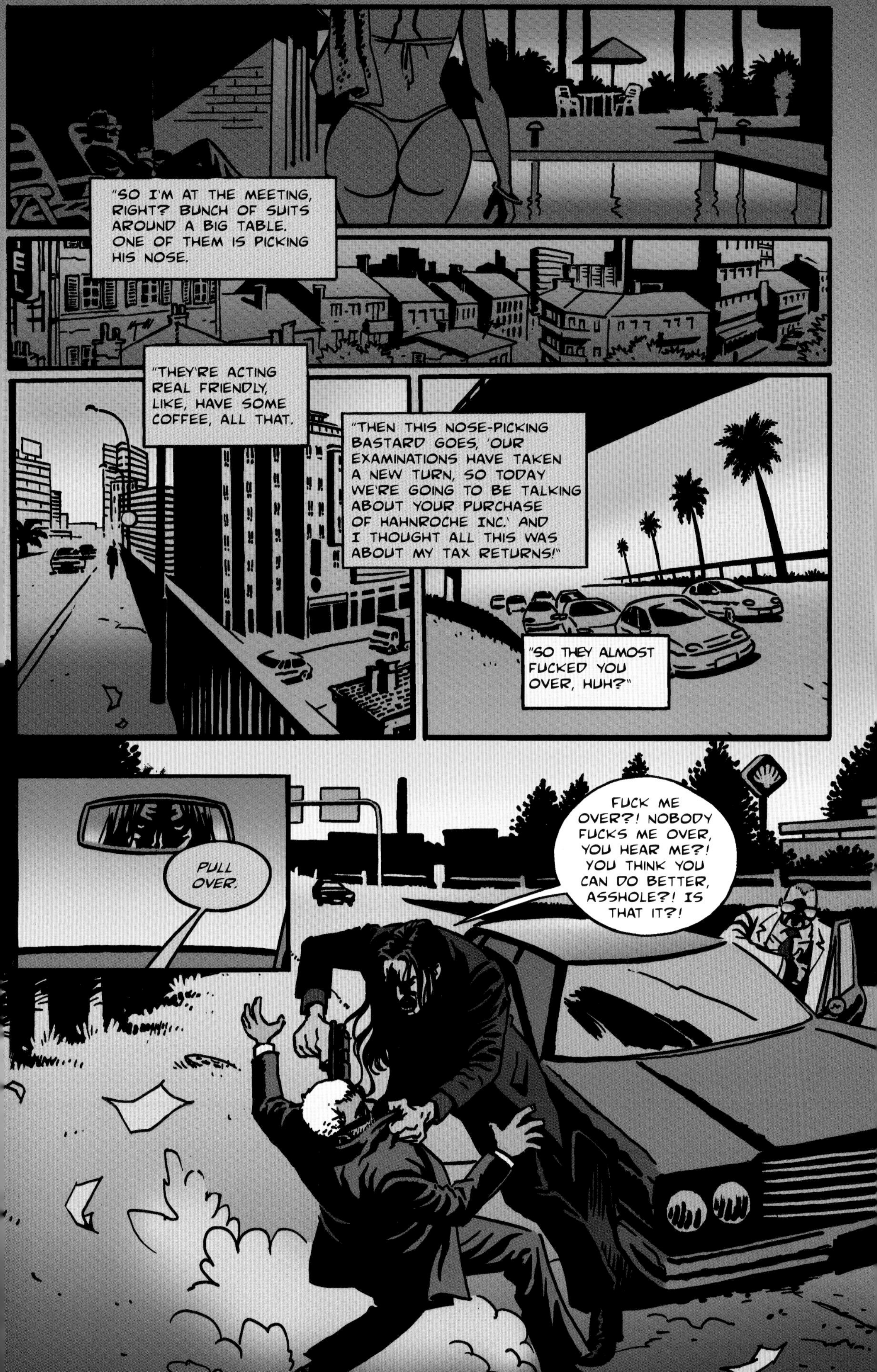
"SO I'M AT THE MEETING, RIGHT? BUNCH OF SUITS AROUND A BIG TABLE. ONE OF THEM IS PICKING HIS NOSE.
"THEY'RE ACTING REAL FRIENDLY, LIKE, HAVE SOME COFFEE, ALL THAT.
"THEN THIS NOSE-PICKING BASTARD GOES, 'OUR EXAMINATIONS HAVE TAKEN A NEW TURN, SO TODAY WE'RE GOING TO BE TALKING ABOUT YOUR PURCHASE OF HAHNROCHE INC.' AND I THOUGHT ALL THIS WAS ABOUT MY TAX RETURNS!"
"SO THEY ALMOST FUCKED YOU OVER, HUH?"
PULL OVER.
FUCK ME OVER?! NOBODY FUCKS ME OVER, YOU HEAR ME?! YOU THINK YOU CAN DO BETTER, ASSHOLE?! IS THAT IT?!

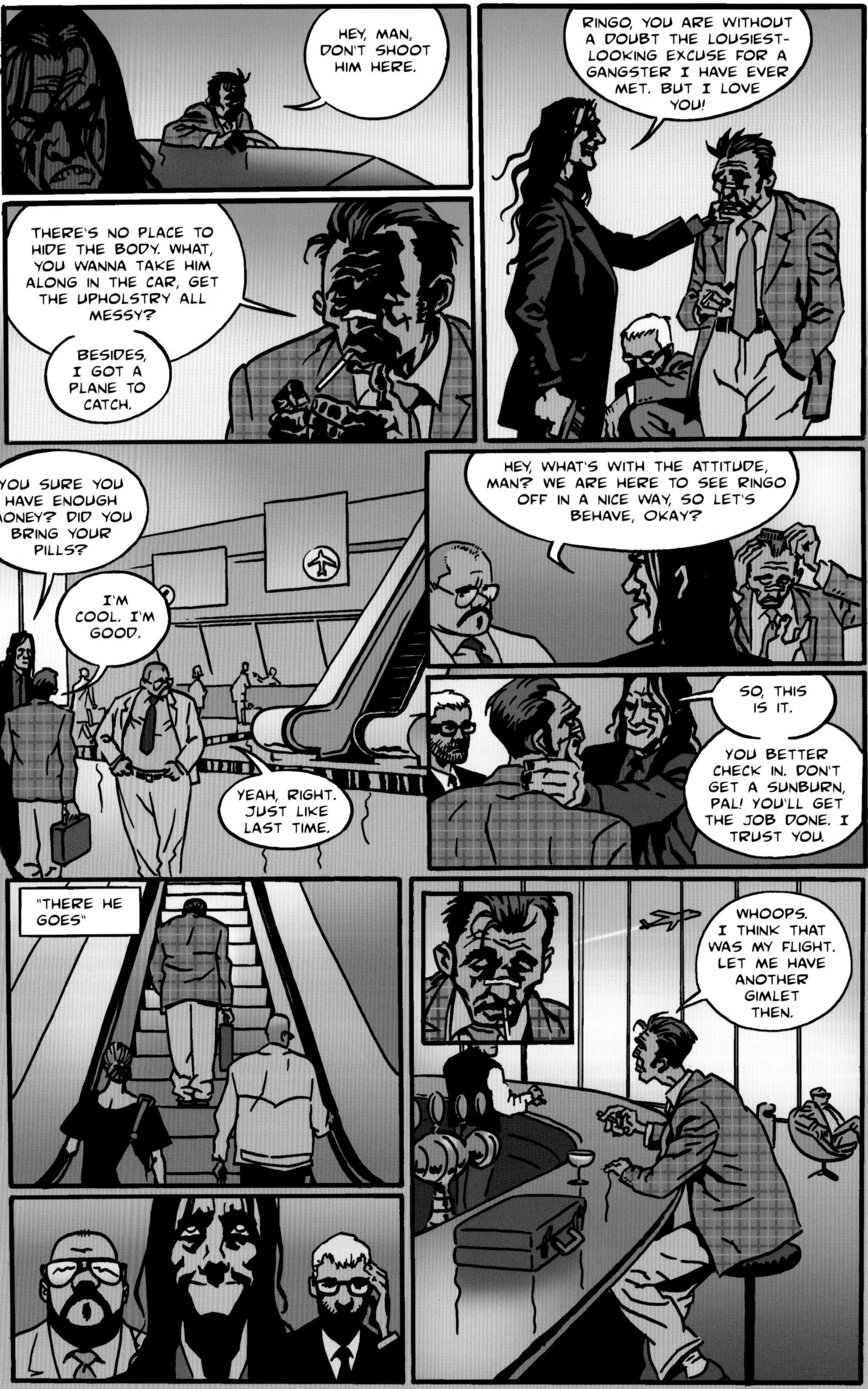
HEY, MAN, DON'T SHOOT HIM HERE.
RINGO, YOU ARE WITHOUT A DOUBT THE LOUSIEST-LOOKING EXCUSE FOR A GANGSTER I HAVE EVER MET. BUT I LOVE YOU!
THERE'S NO PLACE TO HIDE THE BODY. WHAT, YOU WANNA TAKE HIM ALONG IN THE CAR, GET THE UPHOLSTRY ALL MESSY?
BESIDES, I GOT A PLANE TO CATCH.
YOU SURE YOU HAVE ENOUGH MONEY? DID YOU BRING YOUR PILLS?
I'M COOL. I'M GOOD.
YEAH, RIGHT. JUST LIKE LAST TIME.
HEY, WHAT'S WITH THE ATTITUDE, MAN? WE ARE HERE TO SEE RINGO OFF IN A NICE WAY, SO LET'S BEHAVE, OKAY?
SO, THIS IS IT.
YOU BETTER CHECK IN. DON'T GET A SUNBURN, PAL! YOU'LL GET THE JOB DONE. I TRUST YOU.
"THERE HE GOES"
WHOOPS. I THINK THAT WAS MY FLIGHT. LET ME HAVE ANOTHER GIMLET THEN.

PART I

OPPORTUNITY POINT BLANK

"Don't tell me we have to send out an APB for a six-foot clown and a geisha girl."

—Detective Maynard

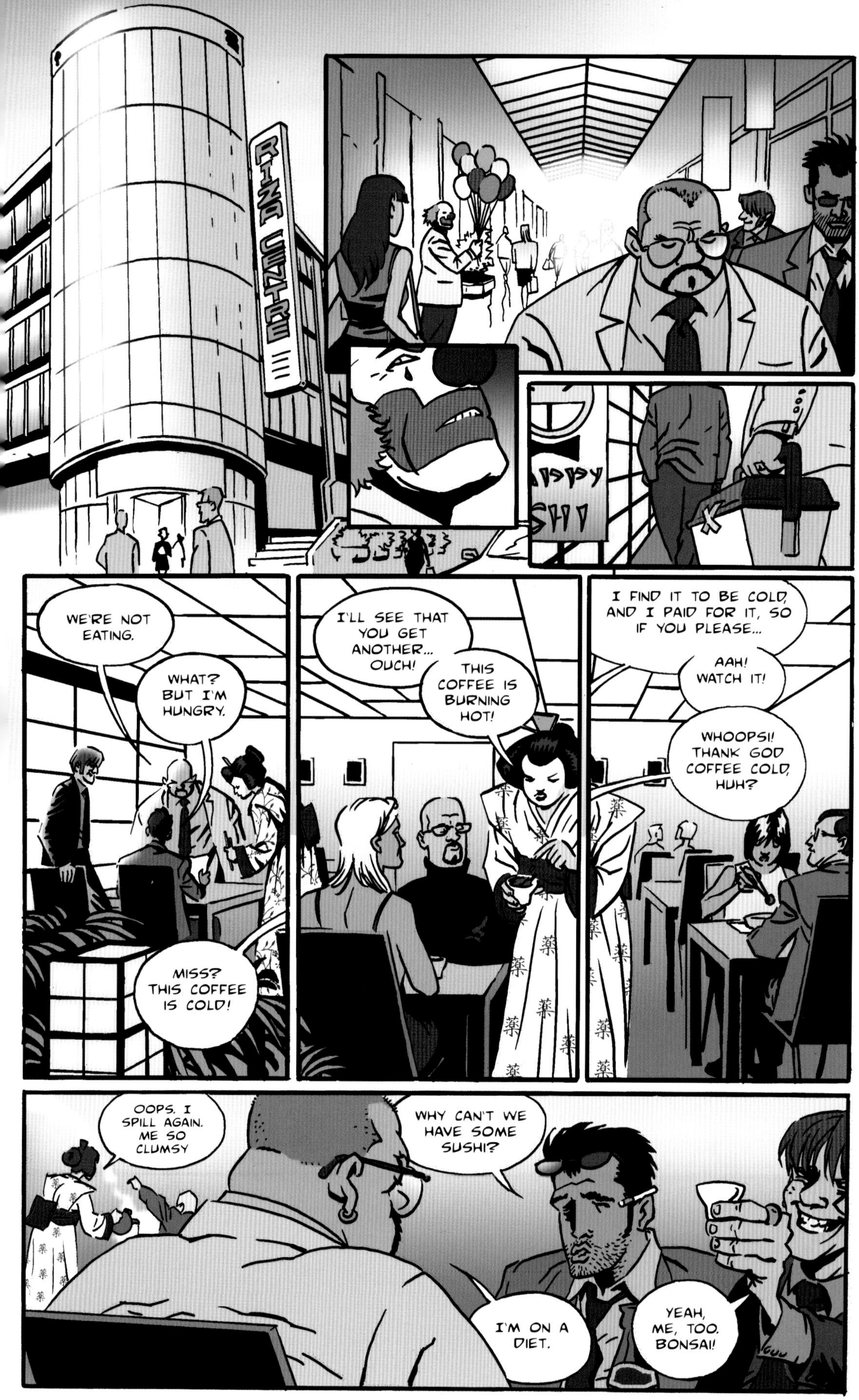
RIZA CENTRE
WE'RE NOT EATING.
WHAT? BUT I'M HUNGRY.
MISS? THIS COFFEE IS COLD!
I'LL SEE THAT YOU GET ANOTHER... OUCH!
THIS COFFEE IS BURNING HOT!
I FIND IT TO BE COLD, AND I PAID FOR IT, SO IF YOU PLEASE...
AAH! WATCH IT!
WHOOPS! THANK GOD COFFEE COLD, HUH?
OOPS. I SPILL AGAIN. ME SO CLUMSY
WHY CAN'T WE HAVE SOME SUSHI?
I'M ON A DIET.
YEAH, ME, TOO. BONSAI!

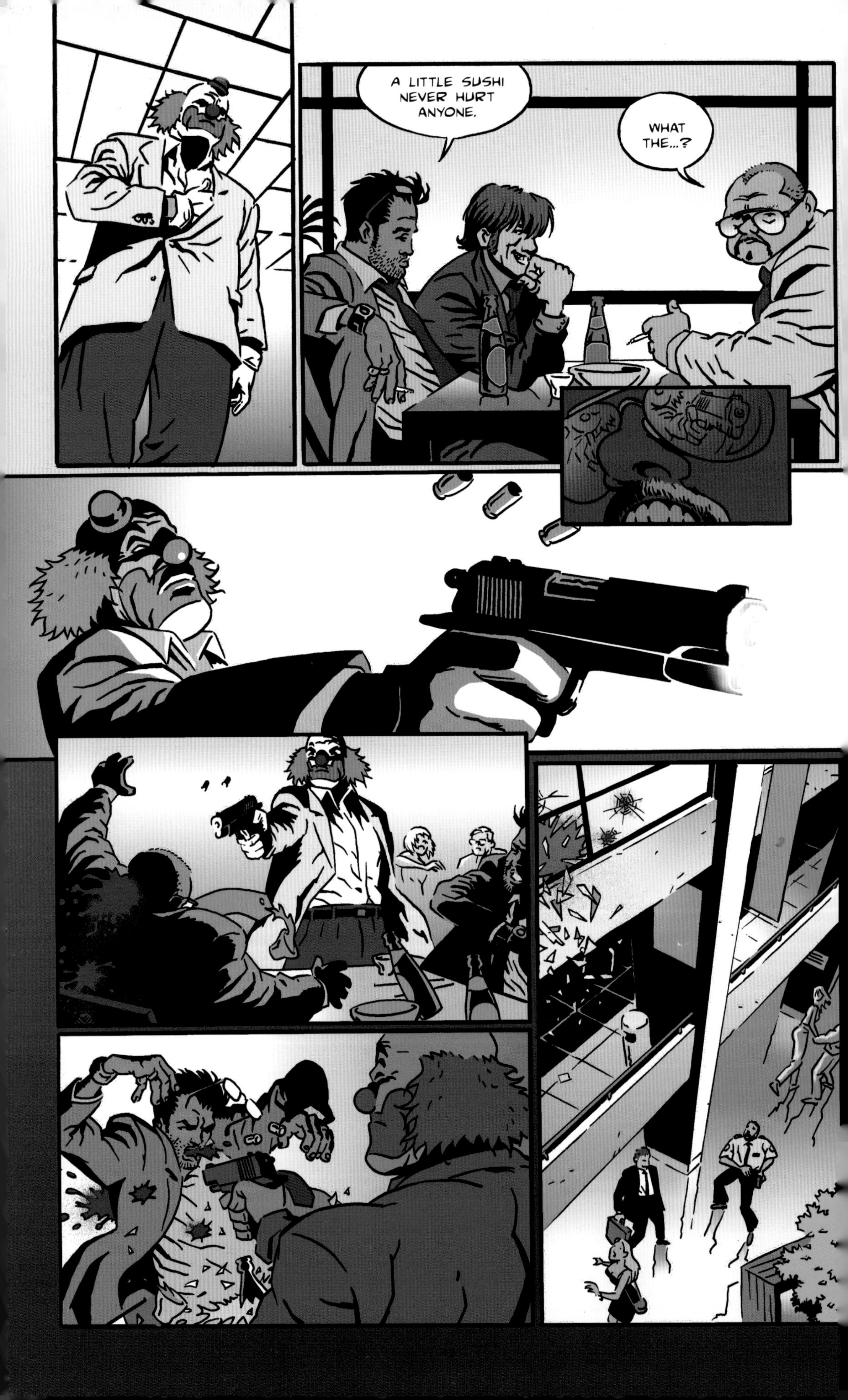
A LITTLE SUSHI NEVER HURT ANYONE.
WHAT THE...?

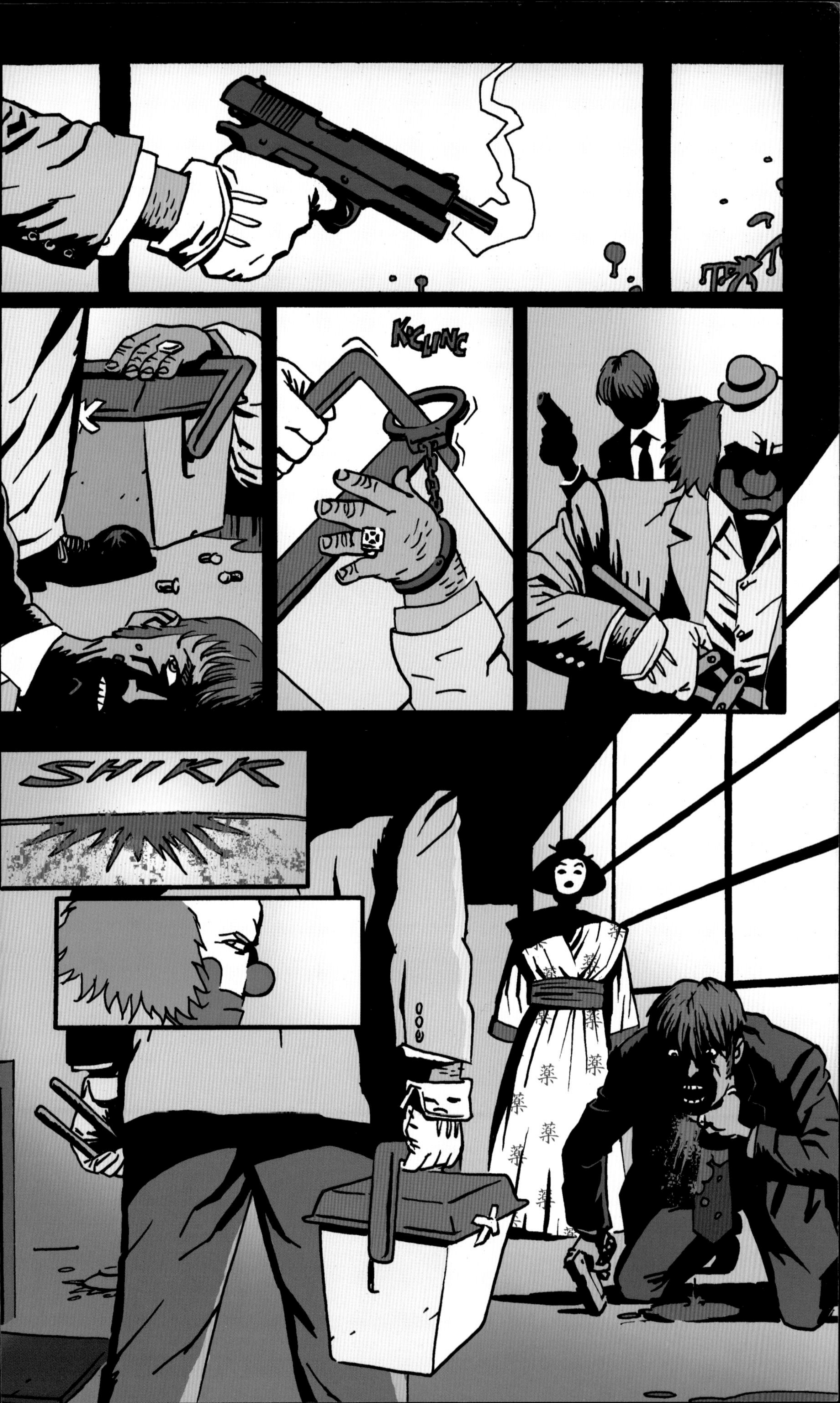
KCLINC
SHIKK

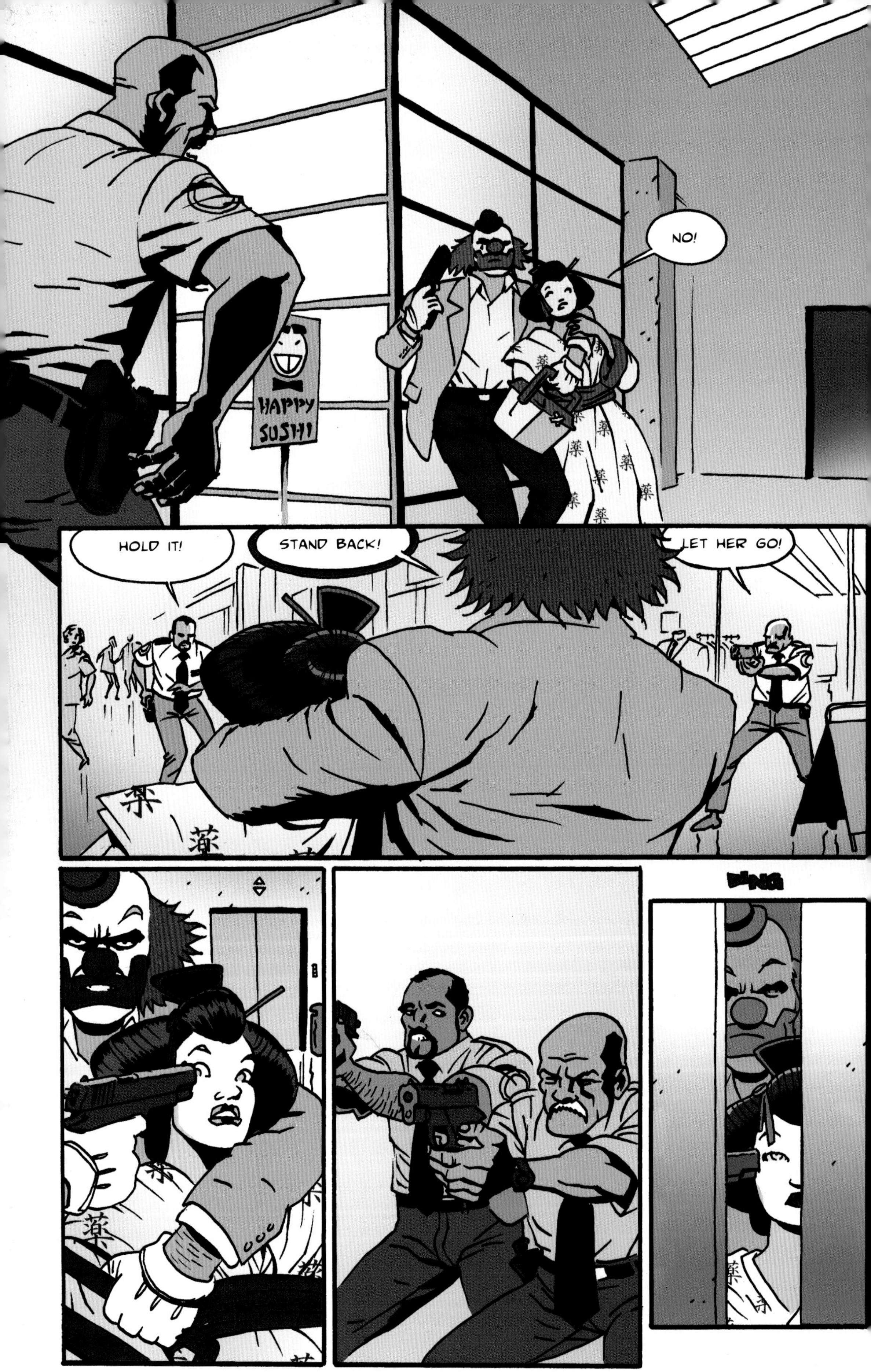

HAPPY SUSHI
NO!
HOLD IT!
STAND BACK!
LET HER GO!
DING

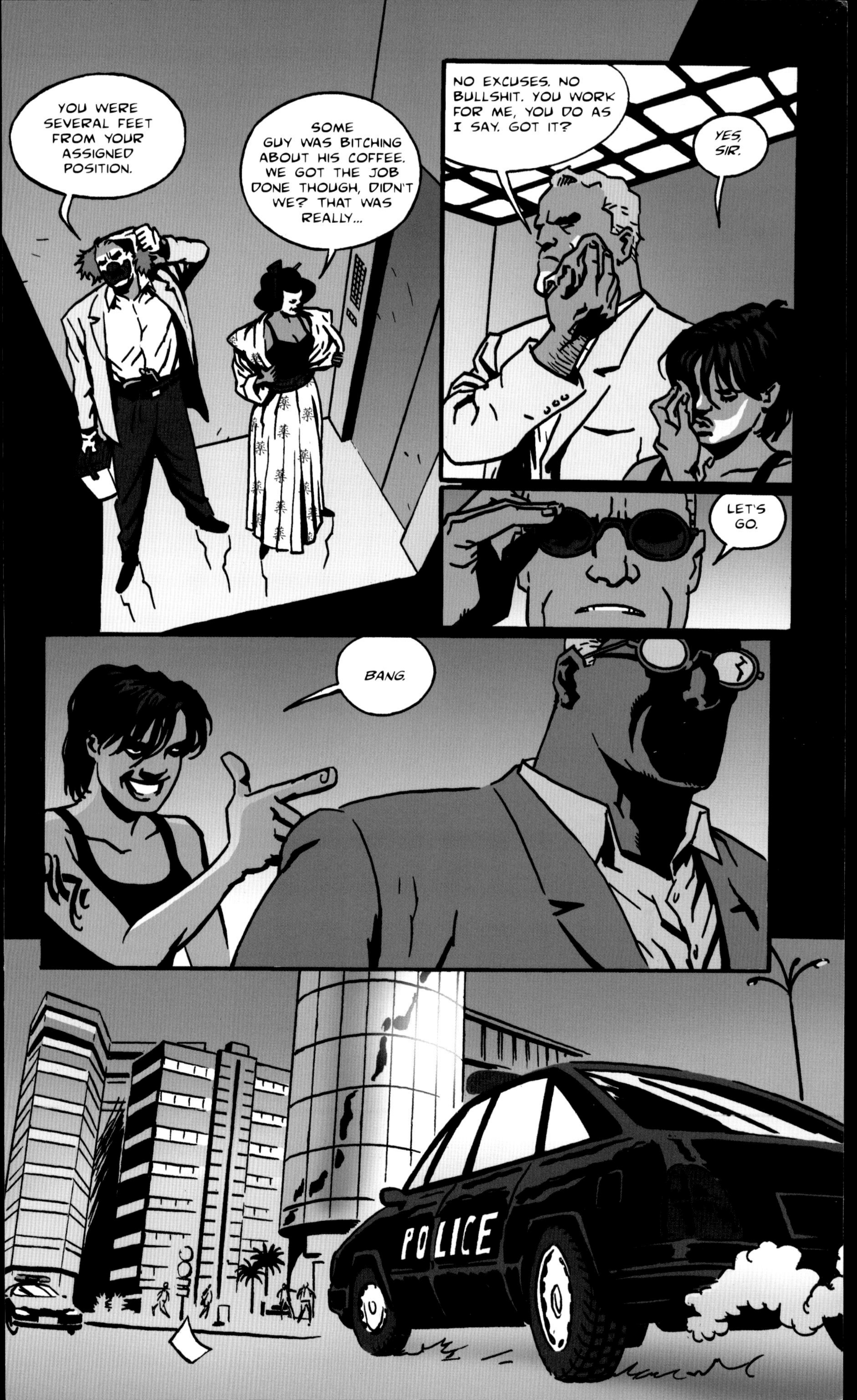
YOU WERE SEVERAL FEET FROM YOUR ASSIGNED POSITION.
SOME GUY WAS BITCHING ABOUT HIS COFFEE. WE GOT THE JOB DONE THOUGH, DIDN'T WE? THAT WAS REALLY...
NO EXCUSES. NO BULLSHIT. YOU WORK FOR ME, YOU DO AS I SAY. GOT IT?
YES, SIR.
LET'S GO.
BANG.
POLICE

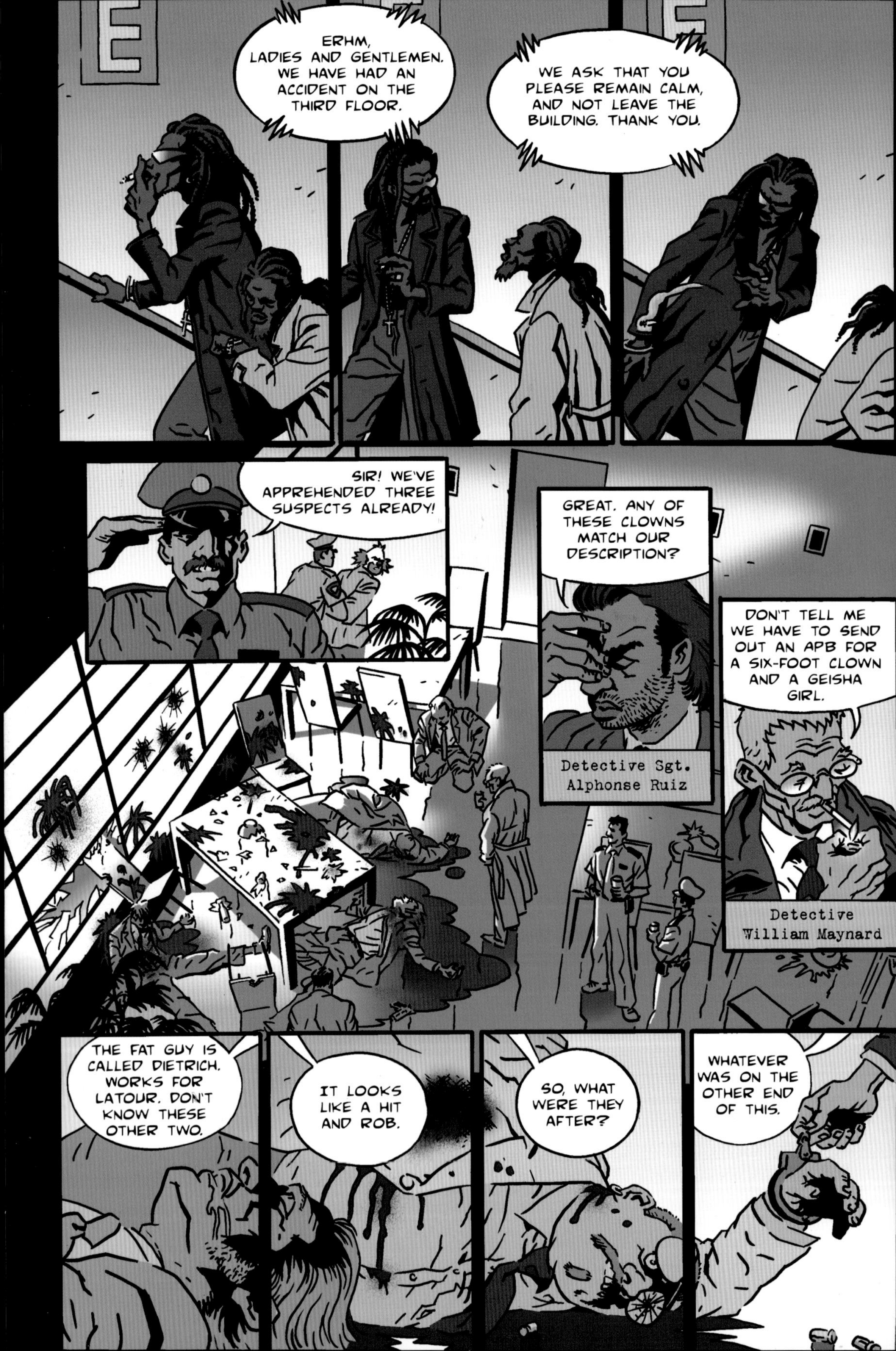
ERHM, LADIES AND GENTLEMEN. WE HAVE HAD AN ACCIDENT ON THE THIRD FLOOR.
WE ASK THAT YOU PLEASE REMAIN CALM, AND NOT LEAVE THE BUILDING. THANK YOU.
SIR! WE'VE APPREHENDED THREE SUSPECTS ALREADY!
GREAT. ANY OF THESE CLOWNS MATCH OUR DESCRIPTION?
Detective Sgt. Alphonse Ruiz
DON'T TELL ME WE HAVE TO SEND OUT AN APB FOR A SIX-FOOT CLOWN AND A GEISHA GIRL.
Detective William Maynard
THE FAT GUY IS CALLED DIETRICH. WORKS FOR LATOUR. DON'T KNOW THESE OTHER TWO.
IT LOOKS LIKE A HIT AND ROB.
SO, WHAT WERE THEY AFTER?
WHATEVER WAS ON THE OTHER END OF THIS.

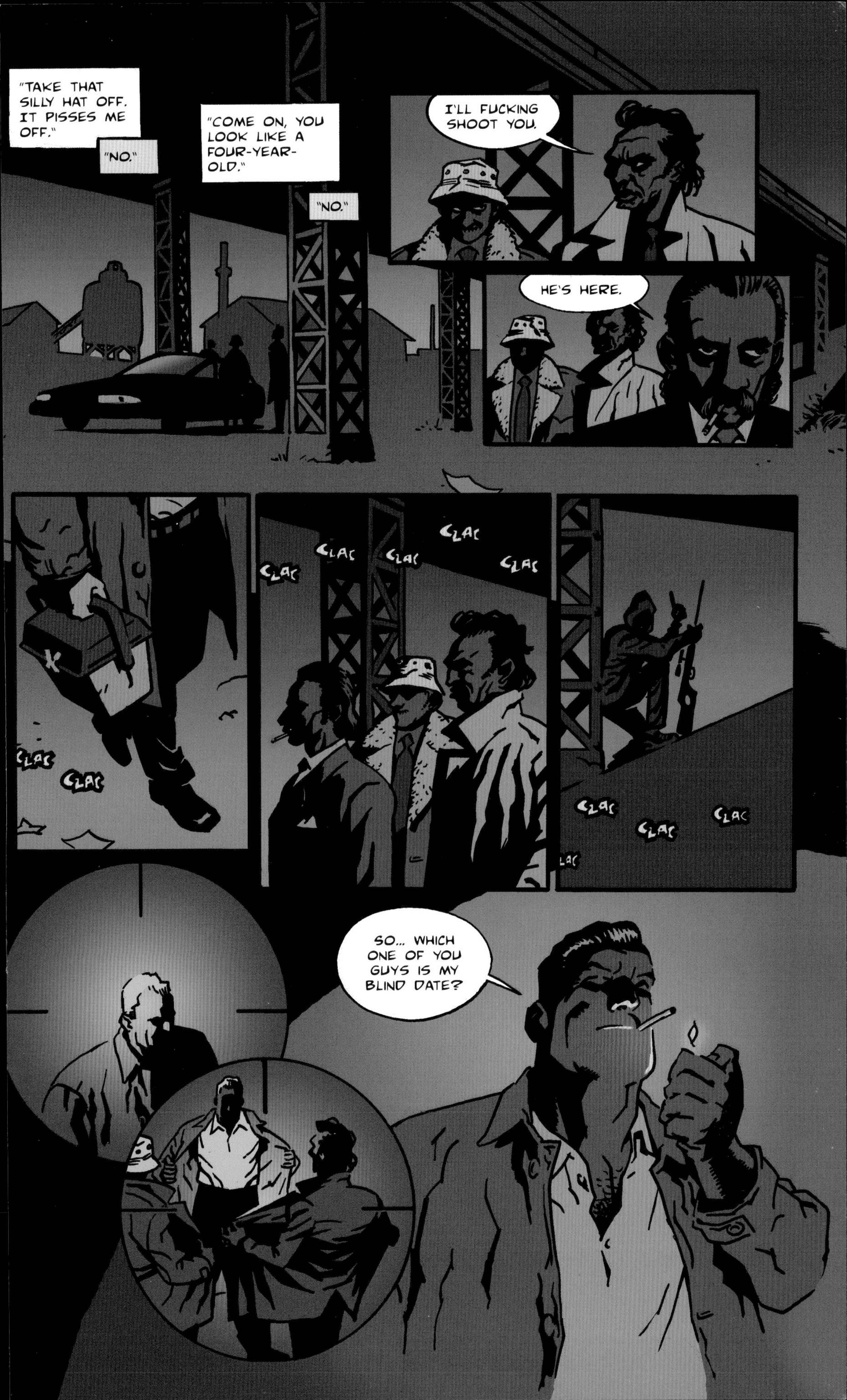
"TAKE THAT SILLY HAT OFF. IT PISSES ME OFF."
"NO."
"COME ON, YOU LOOK LIKE A FOUR-YEAR-OLD."
"NO."
I'LL FUCKING SHOOT YOU.
HE'S HERE.
CLAC
CLAC
CLAC
CLAC
CLAC
CLAC
CLAC
CLAC
CLAC
CLAC
CLAC
SO... WHICH ONE OF YOU GUYS IS MY BLIND DATE?

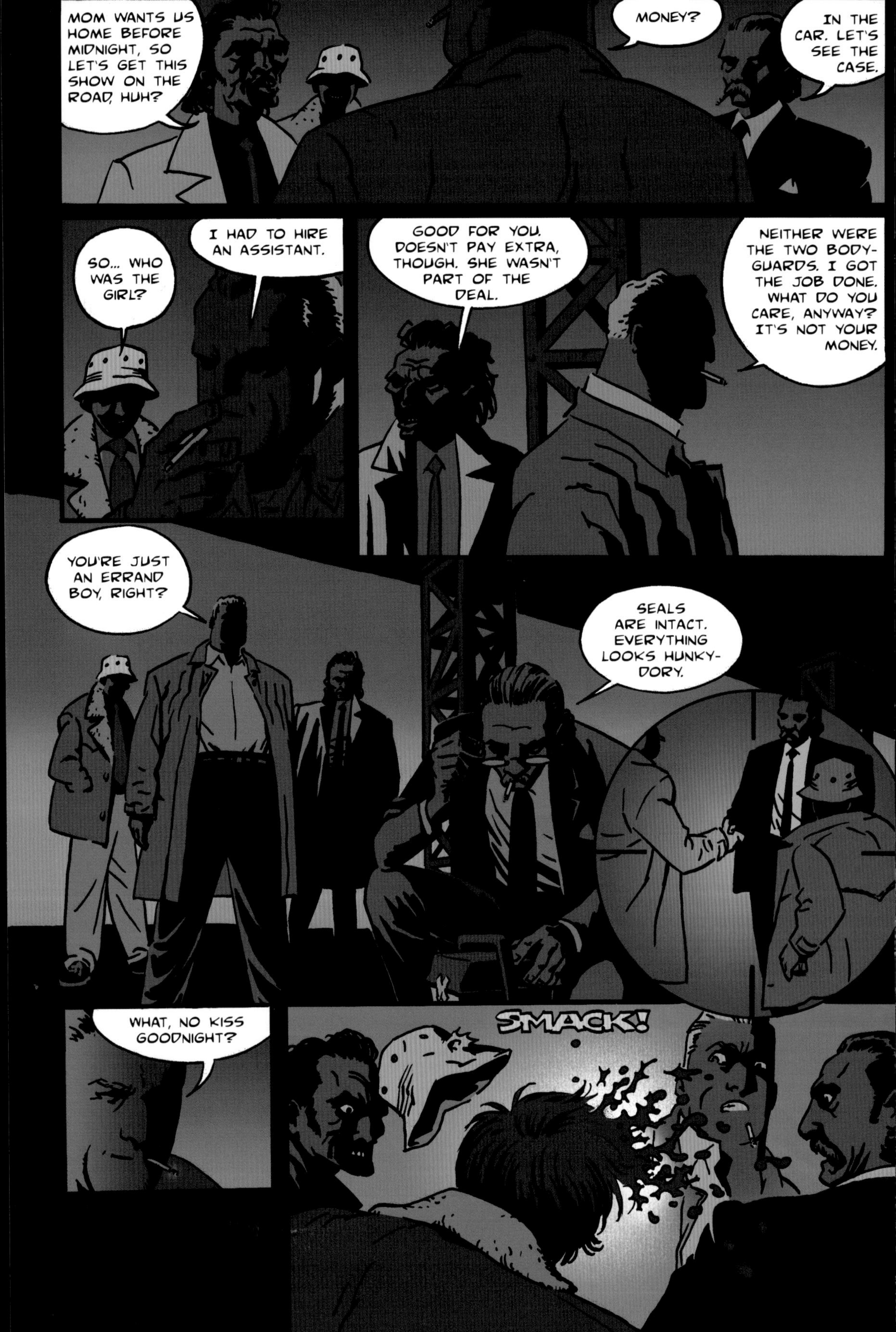
MOM WANTS US HOME BEFORE MIDNIGHT, SO LET'S GET THIS SHOW ON THE ROAD, HUH?
MONEY?
IN THE CAR. LET'S SEE THE CASE.
SO... WHO WAS THE GIRL?
I HAD TO HIRE AN ASSISTANT.
GOOD FOR YOU. DOESN'T PAY EXTRA, THOUGH. SHE WASN'T PART OF THE DEAL.
NEITHER WERE THE TWO BODY-GUARDS. I GOT THE JOB DONE. WHAT DO YOU CARE, ANYWAY? IT'S NOT YOUR MONEY.
YOU'RE JUST AN ERRAND BOY, RIGHT?
SEALS ARE INTACT. EVERYTHING LOOKS HUNKY-DORY.
WHAT, NO KISS GOODNIGHT?
SMACK!

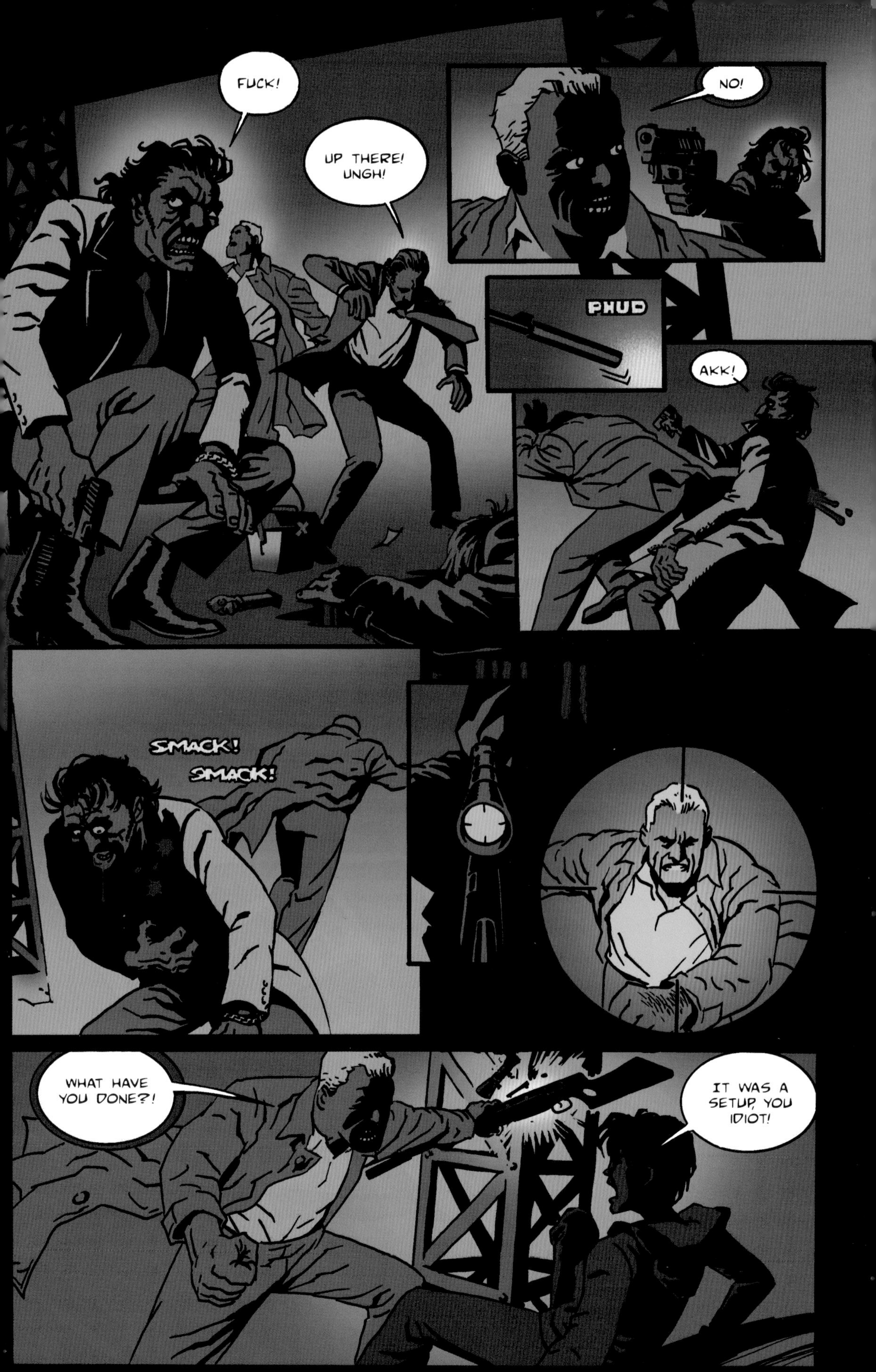
FUCK!
UP THERE! UNGH!
NO!
PHUD
AKK!
SMACK!
SMACK!
WHAT HAVE YOU DONE?!
IT WAS A SETUP, YOU IDIOT!

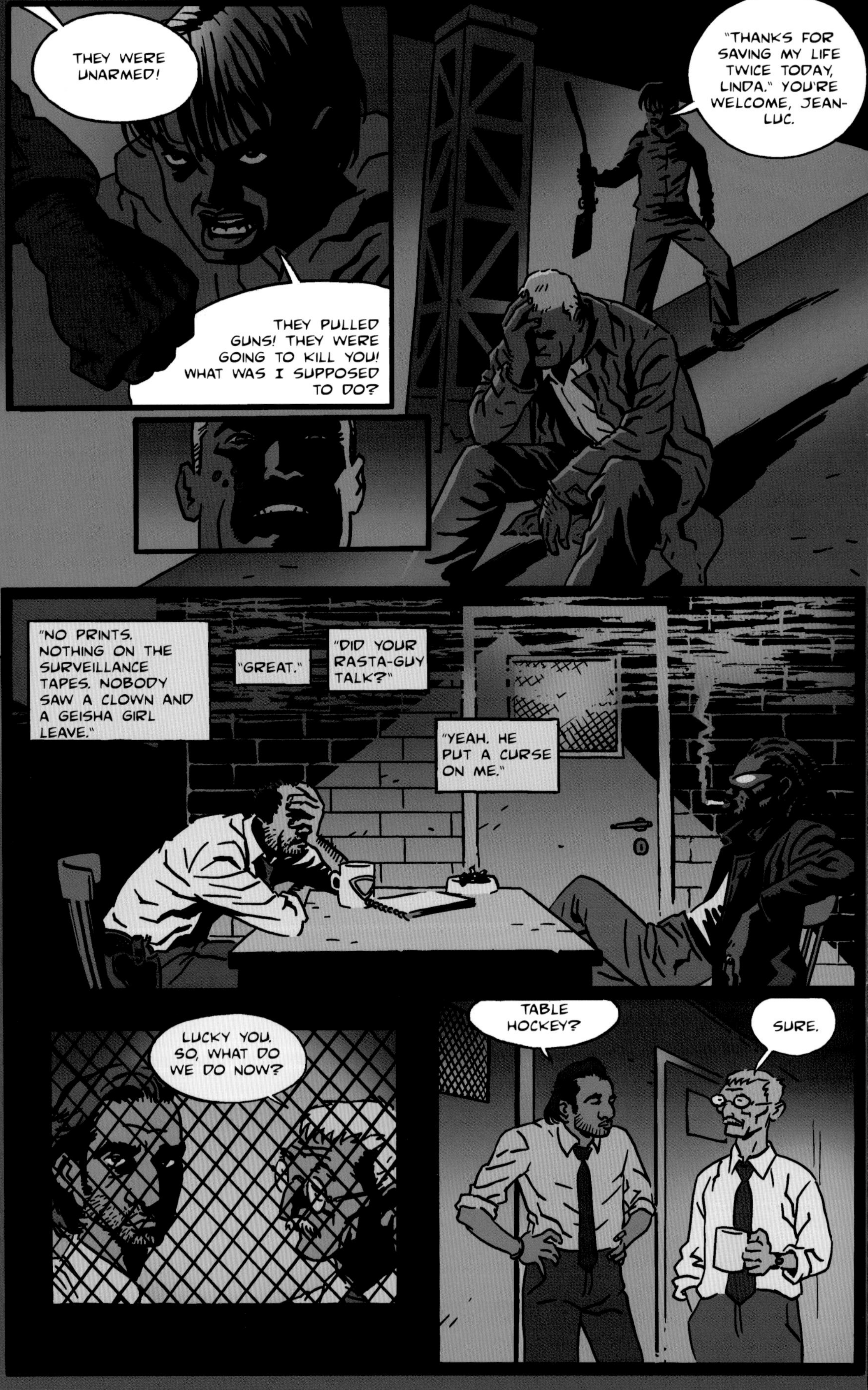
THEY WERE UNARMED!
THEY PULLED GUNS! THEY WERE GOING TO KILL YOU! WHAT WAS I SUPPOSED TO DO?
"THANKS FOR SAVING MY LIFE TWICE TODAY, LINDA." YOU'RE WELCOME, JEAN-LUC.
"NO PRINTS. NOTHING ON THE SURVEILLANCE TAPES. NOBODY SAW A CLOWN AND A GEISHA GIRL LEAVE."
"GREAT."
"DID YOUR RASTA-GUY TALK?"
"YEAH. HE PUT A CURSE ON ME."
LUCKY YOU. SO, WHAT DO WE DO NOW?
TABLE HOCKEY?
SURE.

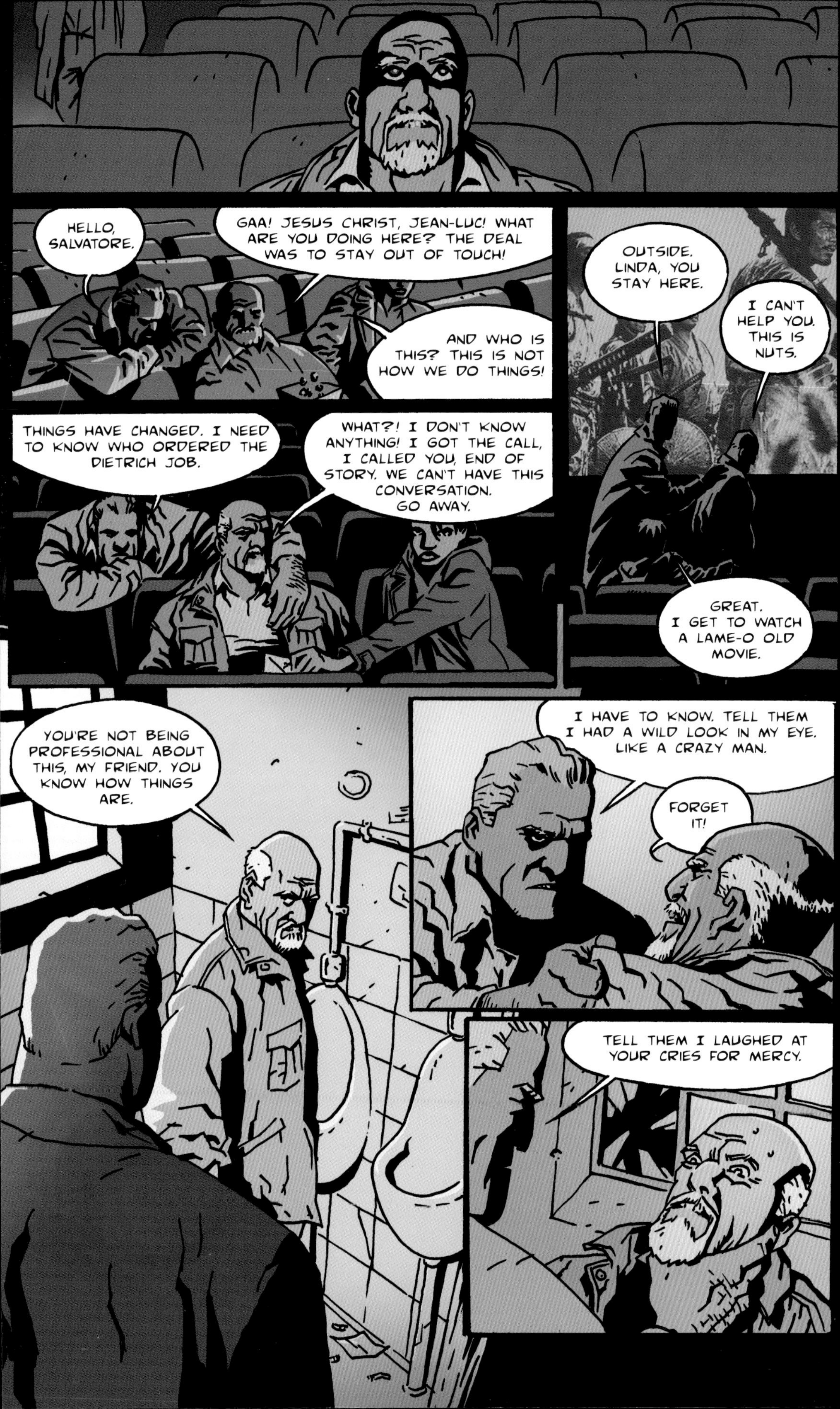
HELLO, SALVATORE.
GAA! JESUS CHRIST, JEAN-LUC! WHAT ARE YOU DOING HERE? THE DEAL WAS TO STAY OUT OF TOUCH!
AND WHO IS THIS? THIS IS NOT HOW WE DO THINGS!
OUTSIDE. LINDA, YOU STAY HERE.
I CAN'T HELP YOU. THIS IS NUTS.
THINGS HAVE CHANGED. I NEED TO KNOW WHO ORDERED THE DIETRICH JOB.
WHAT?! I DON'T KNOW ANYTHING! I GOT THE CALL, I CALLED YOU, END OF STORY. WE CAN'T HAVE THIS CONVERSATION. GO AWAY.
GREAT. I GET TO WATCH A LAME-O OLD MOVIE.
YOU'RE NOT BEING PROFESSIONAL ABOUT THIS, MY FRIEND. YOU KNOW HOW THINGS ARE.
I HAVE TO KNOW. TELL THEM I HAD A WILD LOOK IN MY EYE. LIKE A CRAZY MAN.
FORGET IT!
TELL THEM I LAUGHED AT YOUR CRIES FOR MERCY.

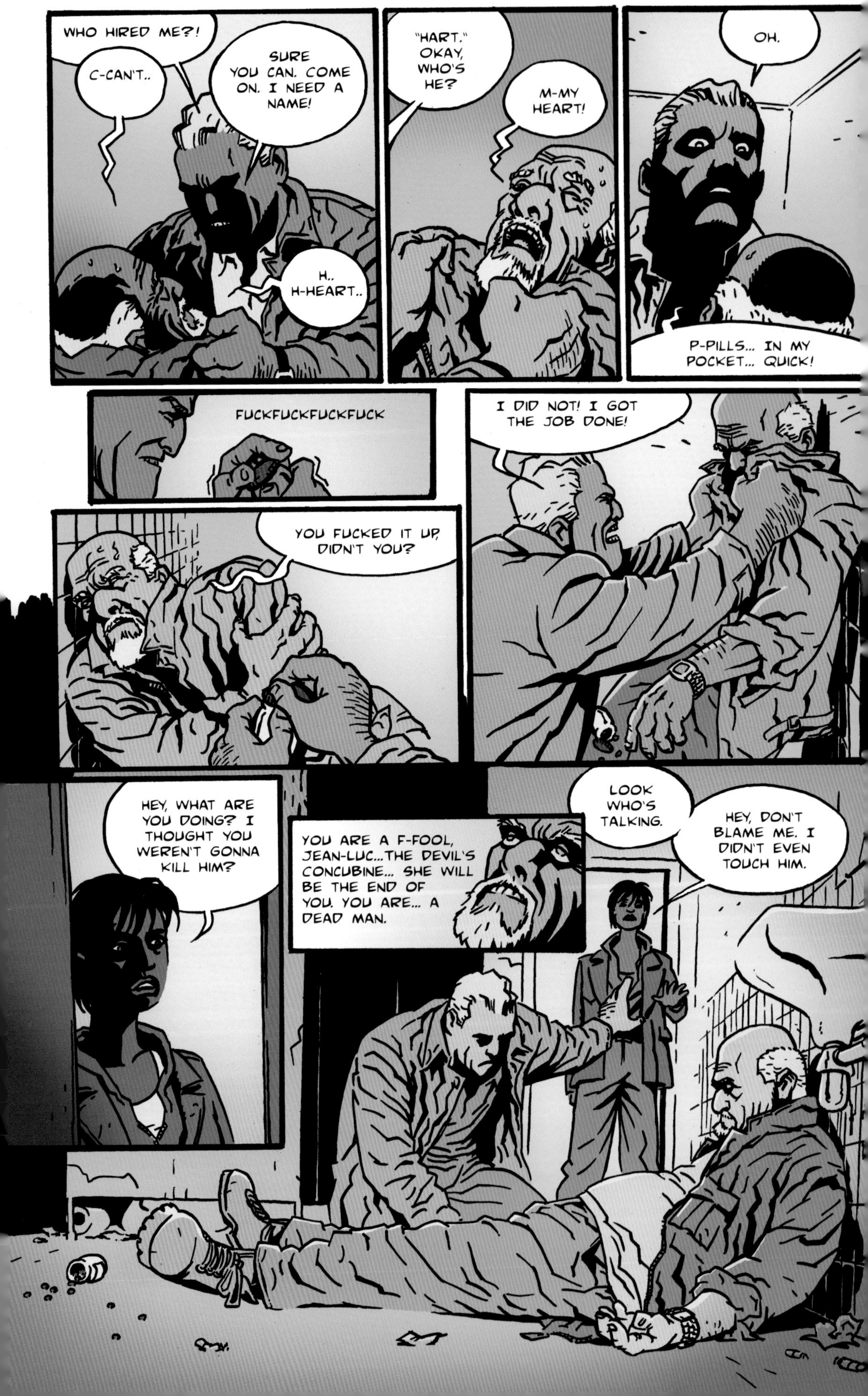
WHO HIRED ME?!
C-CAN'T..
SURE YOU CAN. COME ON. I NEED A NAME!
H.. H-HEART..
"HART." OKAY, WHO'S HE?
M-MY HEART!
OH.
P-PILLS... IN MY POCKET... QUICK!
FUCKFUCKFUCKFUCK
YOU FUCKED IT UP, DIDN'T YOU?
I DID NOT! I GOT THE JOB DONE!
HEY, WHAT ARE YOU DOING? I THOUGHT YOU WEREN'T GONNA KILL HIM?
YOU ARE A F-FOOL, JEAN-LUC...THE DEVIL'S CONCUBINE... SHE WILL BE THE END OF YOU. YOU ARE... A DEAD MAN.
LOOK WHO'S TALKING.
HEY, DON'T BLAME ME. I DIDN'T EVEN TOUCH HIM.

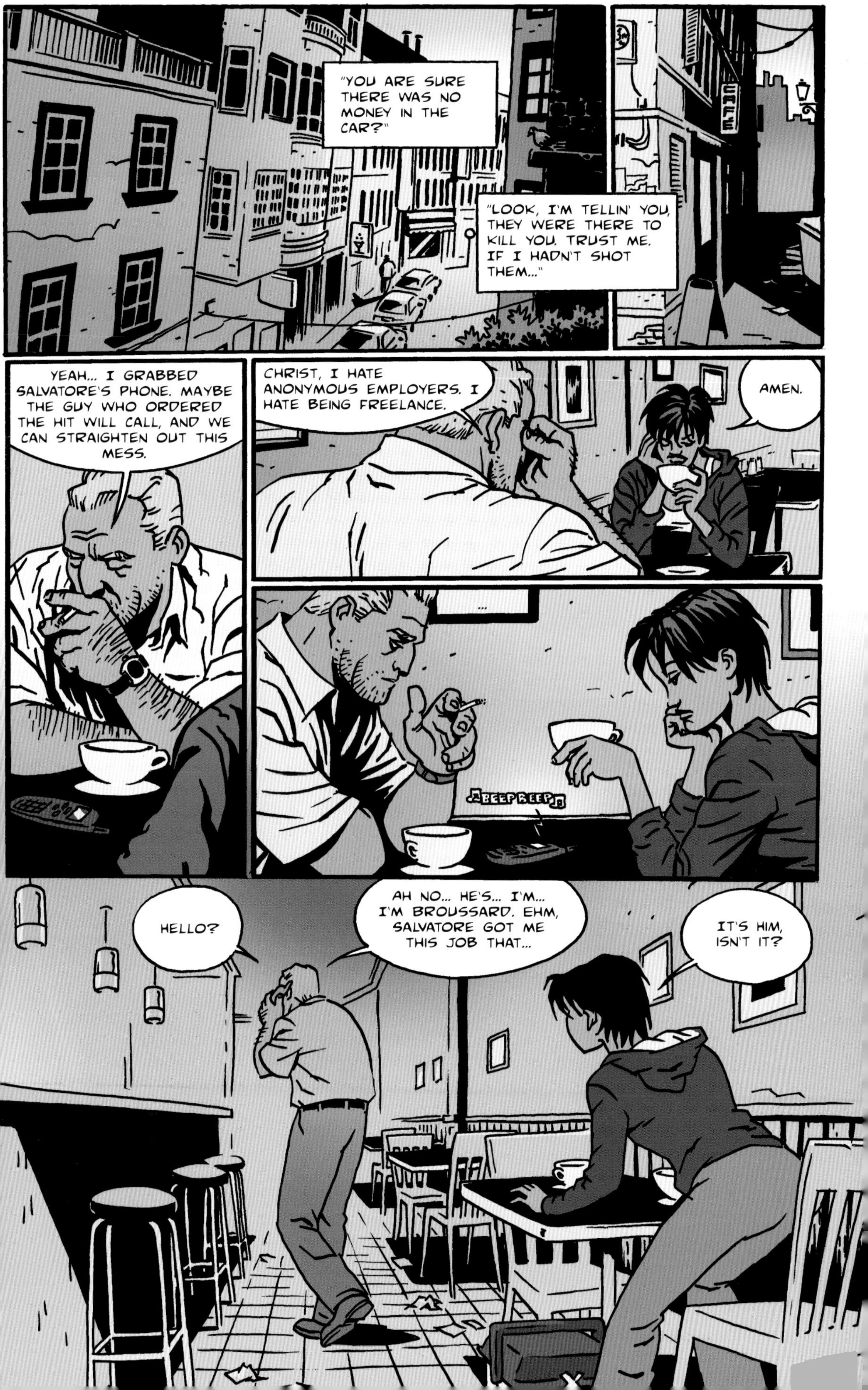
"YOU ARE SURE THERE WAS NO MONEY IN THE CAR?"
"LOOK, I'M TELLIN' YOU, THEY WERE THERE TO KILL YOU. TRUST ME. IF I HADN'T SHOT THEM..."
CAFE
YEAH... I GRABBED SALVATORE'S PHONE. MAYBE THE GUY WHO ORDERED THE HIT WILL CALL, AND WE CAN STRAIGHTEN OUT THIS MESS.
CHRIST, I HATE ANONYMOUS EMPLOYERS. I HATE BEING FREELANCE.
AMEN.
...
BEEP BEEP
HELLO?
AH NO... HE'S... I'M... I'M BROUSSARD. EHM, SALVATORE GOT ME THIS JOB THAT...
IT'S HIM, ISN'T IT?

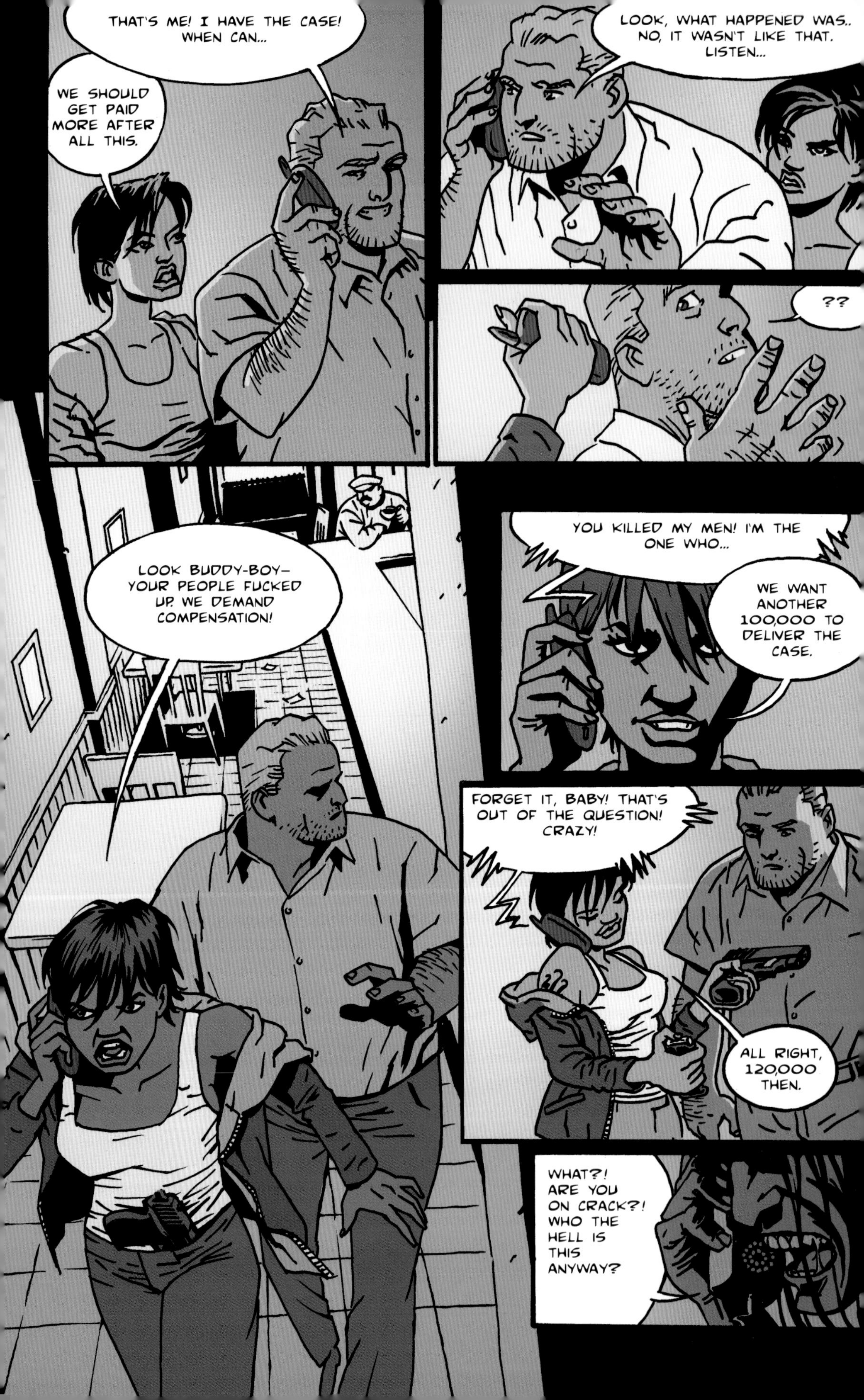
THAT'S ME! I HAVE THE CASE! WHEN CAN...
WE SHOULD GET PAID MORE AFTER ALL THIS.
LOOK, WHAT HAPPENED WAS.. NO, IT WASN'T LIKE THAT. LISTEN...
??
LOOK BUDDY-BOY– YOUR PEOPLE FUCKED UP. WE DEMAND COMPENSATION!
YOU KILLED MY MEN! I'M THE ONE WHO...
WE WANT ANOTHER 100,000 TO DELIVER THE CASE.
FORGET IT, BABY! THAT'S OUT OF THE QUESTION! CRAZY!
ALL RIGHT, 120,000 THEN.
WHAT?! ARE YOU ON CRACK?! WHO THE HELL IS THIS ANYWAY?

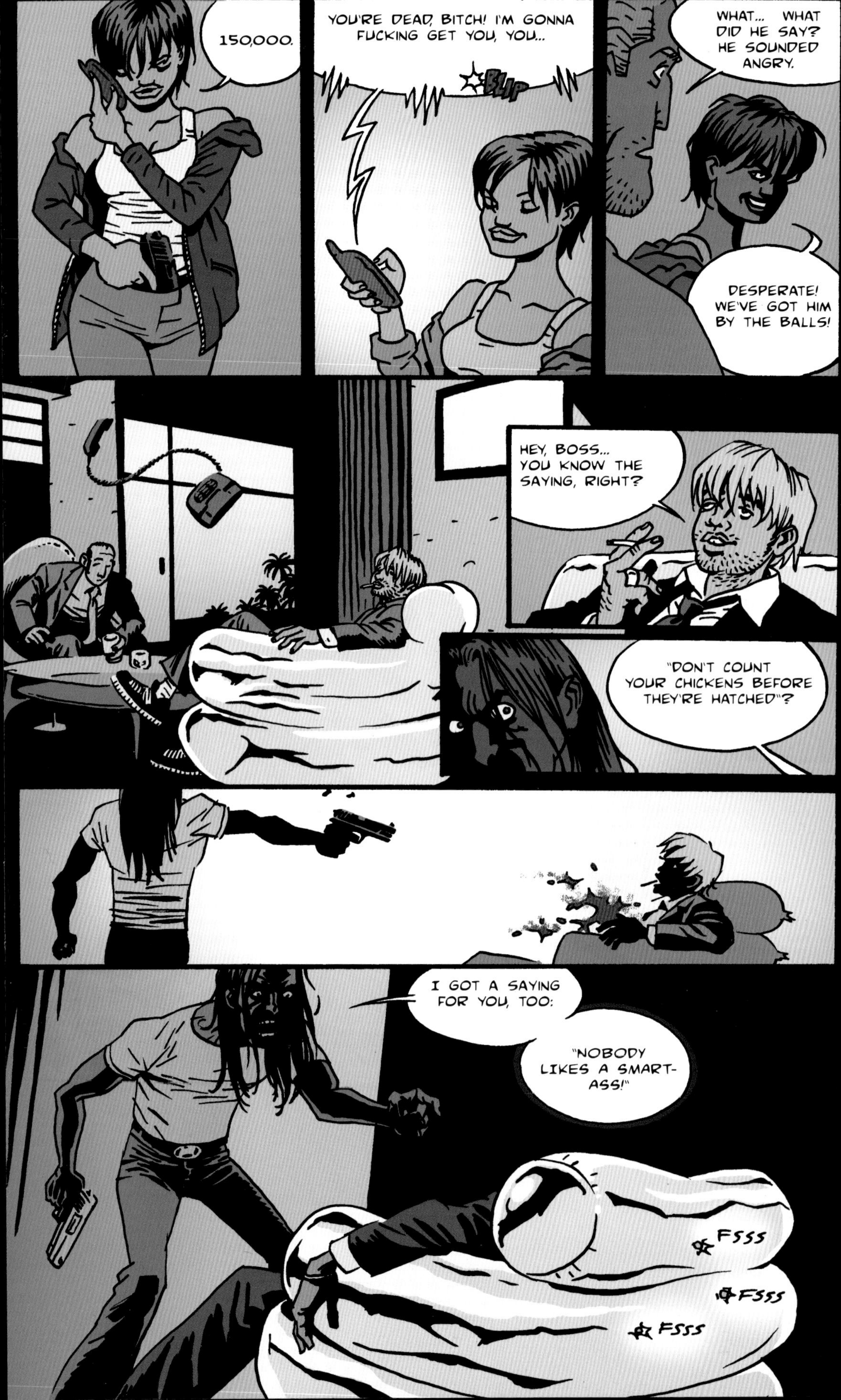
150,000.
YOU'RE DEAD, BITCH! I'M GONNA FUCKING GET YOU, YOU...
BLIP
WHAT... WHAT DID HE SAY? HE SOUNDED ANGRY.
DESPERATE! WE'VE GOT HIM BY THE BALLS!
HEY, BOSS... YOU KNOW THE SAYING, RIGHT?
"DON'T COUNT YOUR CHICKENS BEFORE THEY'RE HATCHED"?
I GOT A SAYING FOR YOU, TOO:
"NOBODY LIKES A SMART-ASS!"
FSSS
FSSS
FSSS

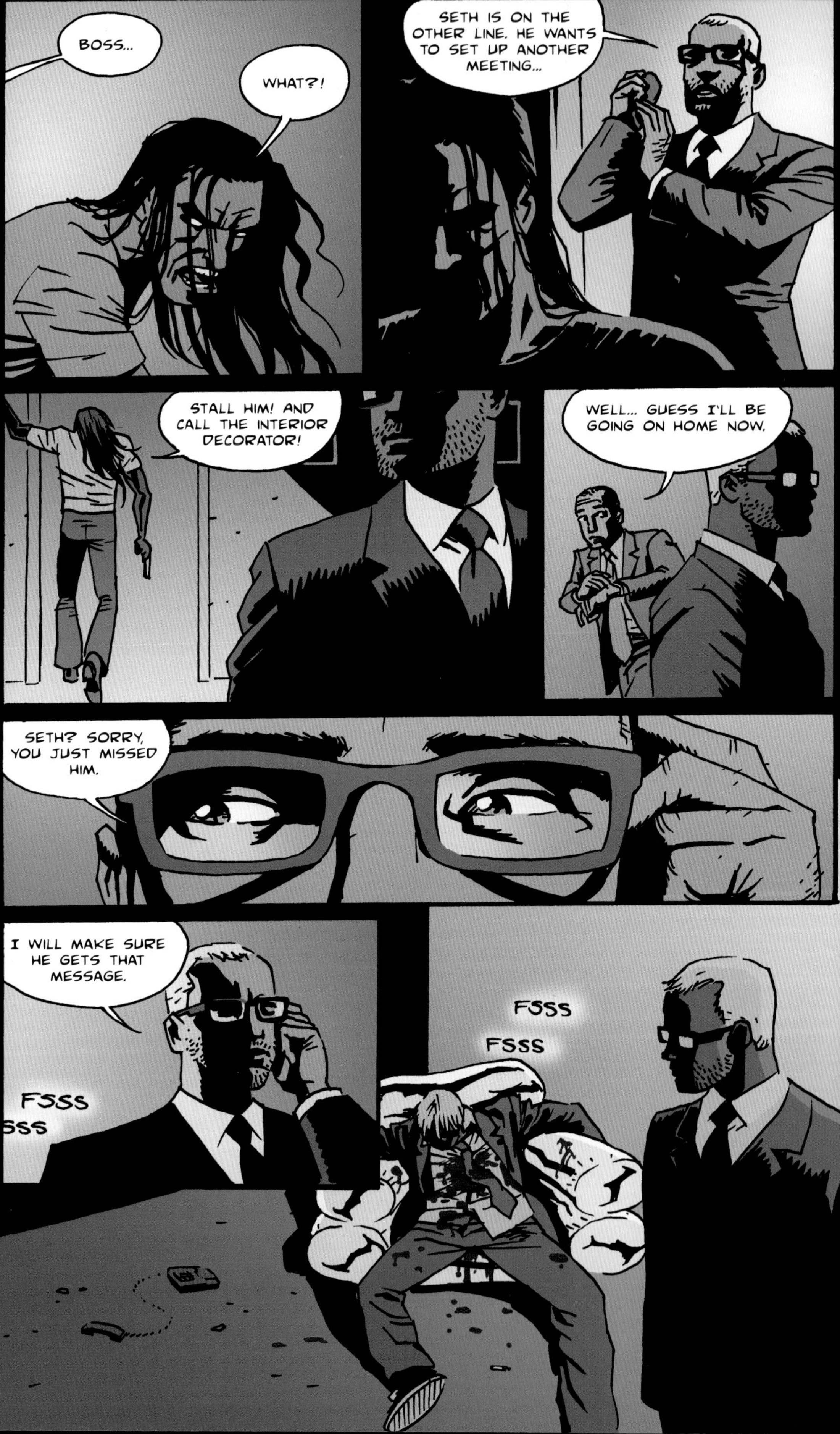

BOSS...
WHAT?!
SETH IS ON THE OTHER LINE. HE WANTS TO SET UP ANOTHER MEETING...
STALL HIM! AND CALL THE INTERIOR DECORATOR!
WELL... GUESS I'LL BE GOING ON HOME NOW.
SETH? SORRY, YOU JUST MISSED HIM.
I WILL MAKE SURE HE GETS THAT MESSAGE.
FSSS
SSS
FSSS
FSSS

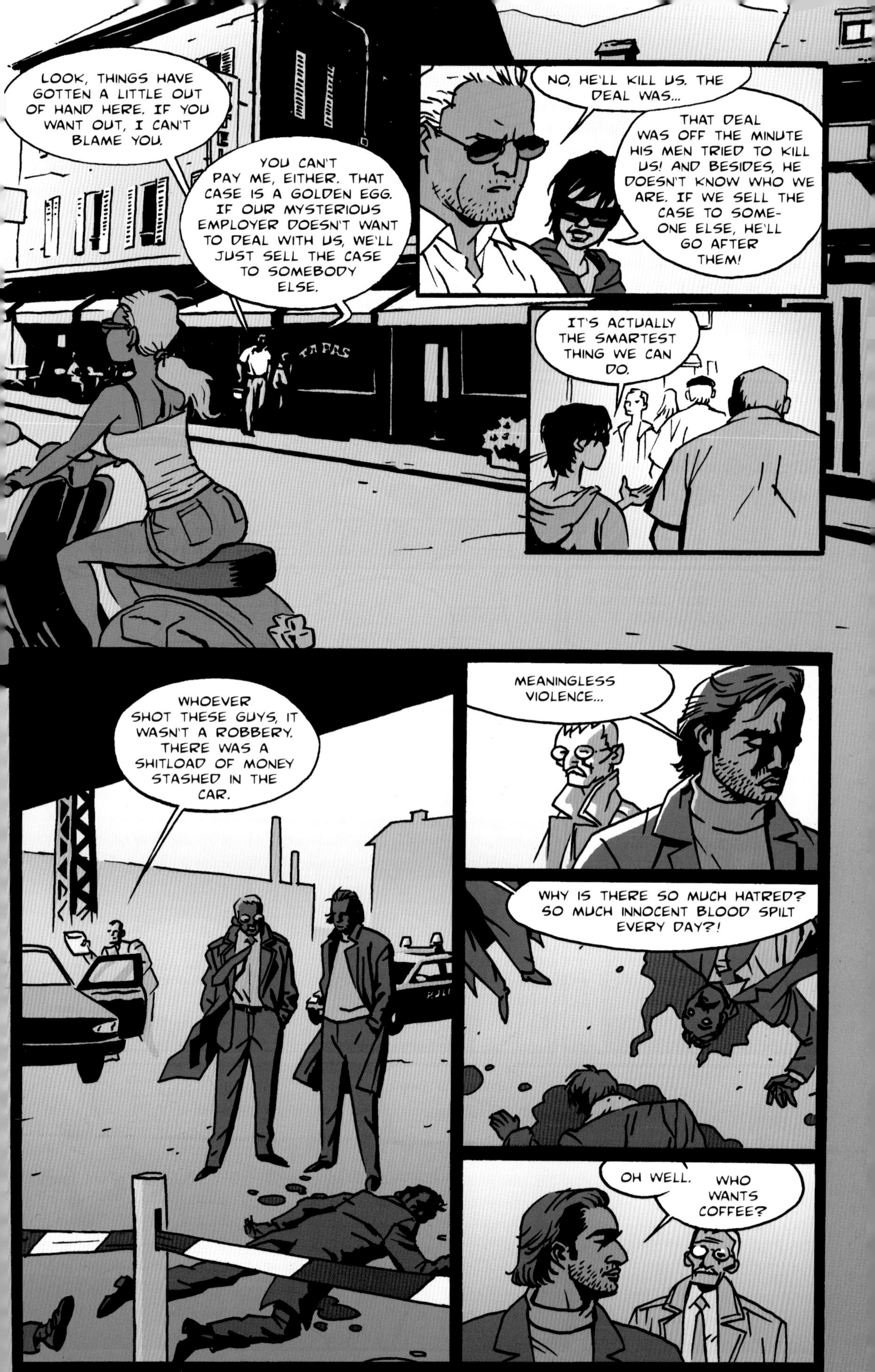
LOOK, THINGS HAVE GOTTEN A LITTLE OUT OF HAND HERE. IF YOU WANT OUT, I CAN'T BLAME YOU.
YOU CAN'T PAY ME, EITHER. THAT CASE IS A GOLDEN EGG. IF OUR MYSTERIOUS EMPLOYER DOESN'T WANT TO DEAL WITH US, WE'LL JUST SELL THE CASE TO SOMEBODY ELSE.
TAPAS
NO, HE'LL KILL US. THE DEAL WAS...
THAT DEAL WAS OFF THE MINUTE HIS MEN TRIED TO KILL US! AND BESIDES, HE DOESN'T KNOW WHO WE ARE. IF WE SELL THE CASE TO SOMEONE ELSE, HE'LL GO AFTER THEM!
IT'S ACTUALLY THE SMARTEST THING WE CAN DO.
WHOEVER SHOT THESE GUYS, IT WASN'T A ROBBERY. THERE WAS A SHITLOAD OF MONEY STASHED IN THE CAR.
MEANINGLESS VIOLENCE...
WHY IS THERE SO MUCH HATRED? SO MUCH INNOCENT BLOOD SPILT EVERY DAY?!
OH WELL.
WHO WANTS COFFEE?

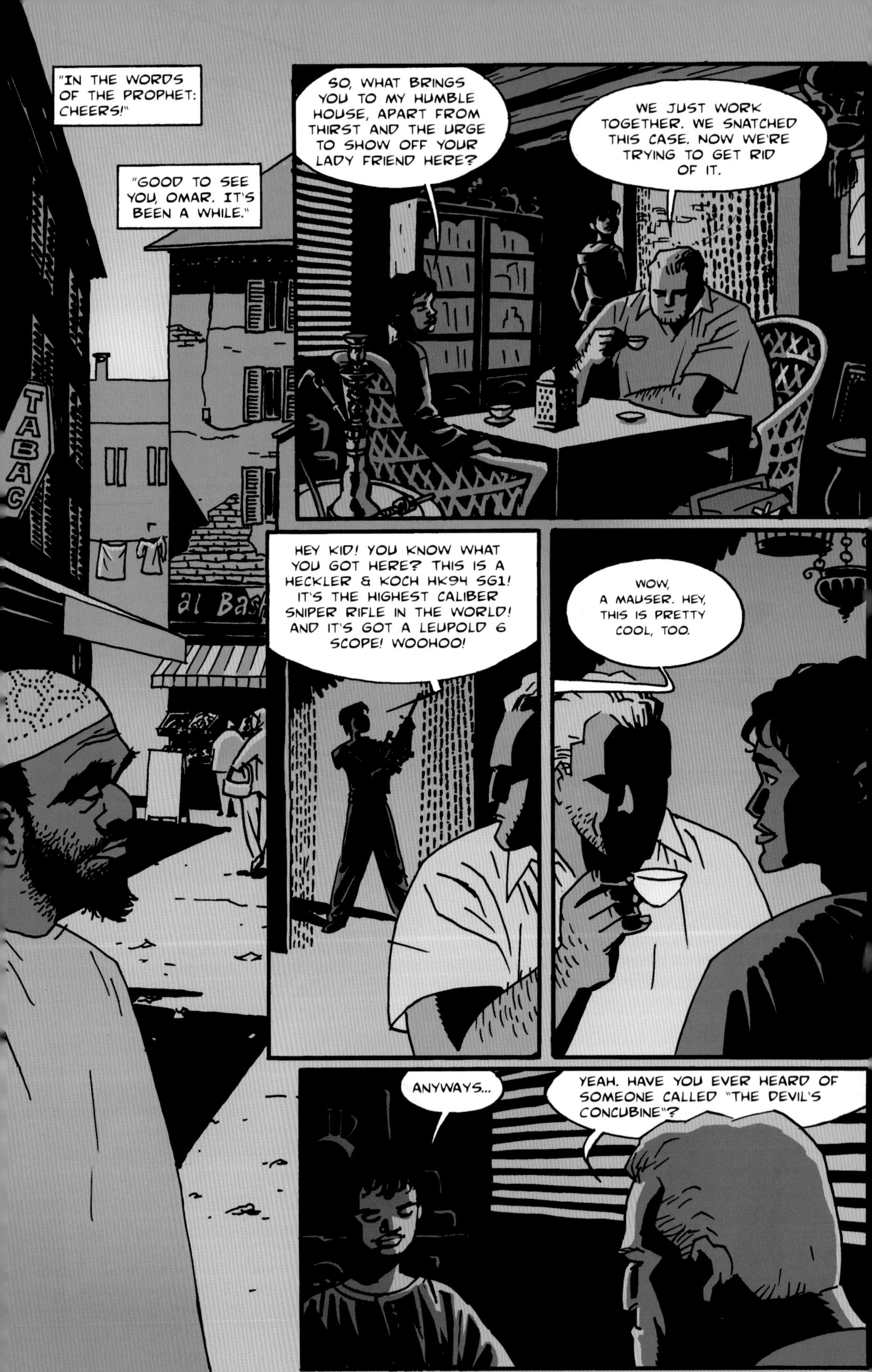
"IN THE WORDS OF THE PROPHET: CHEERS!"
"GOOD TO SEE YOU, OMAR. IT'S BEEN A WHILE."
TABAC
al Bash
SO, WHAT BRINGS YOU TO MY HUMBLE HOUSE, APART FROM THIRST AND THE URGE TO SHOW OFF YOUR LADY FRIEND HERE?
WE JUST WORK TOGETHER. WE SNATCHED THIS CASE. NOW WE'RE TRYING TO GET RID OF IT.
HEY KID! YOU KNOW WHAT YOU GOT HERE? THIS IS A HECKLER & KOCH HK94 SG1! IT'S THE HIGHEST CALIBER SNIPER RIFLE IN THE WORLD! AND IT'S GOT A LEUPOLD 6 SCOPE! WOOHOO!
WOW, A MAUSER. HEY, THIS IS PRETTY COOL, TOO.
ANYWAYS...
YEAH. HAVE YOU EVER HEARD OF SOMEONE CALLED "THE DEVIL'S CONCUBINE"?

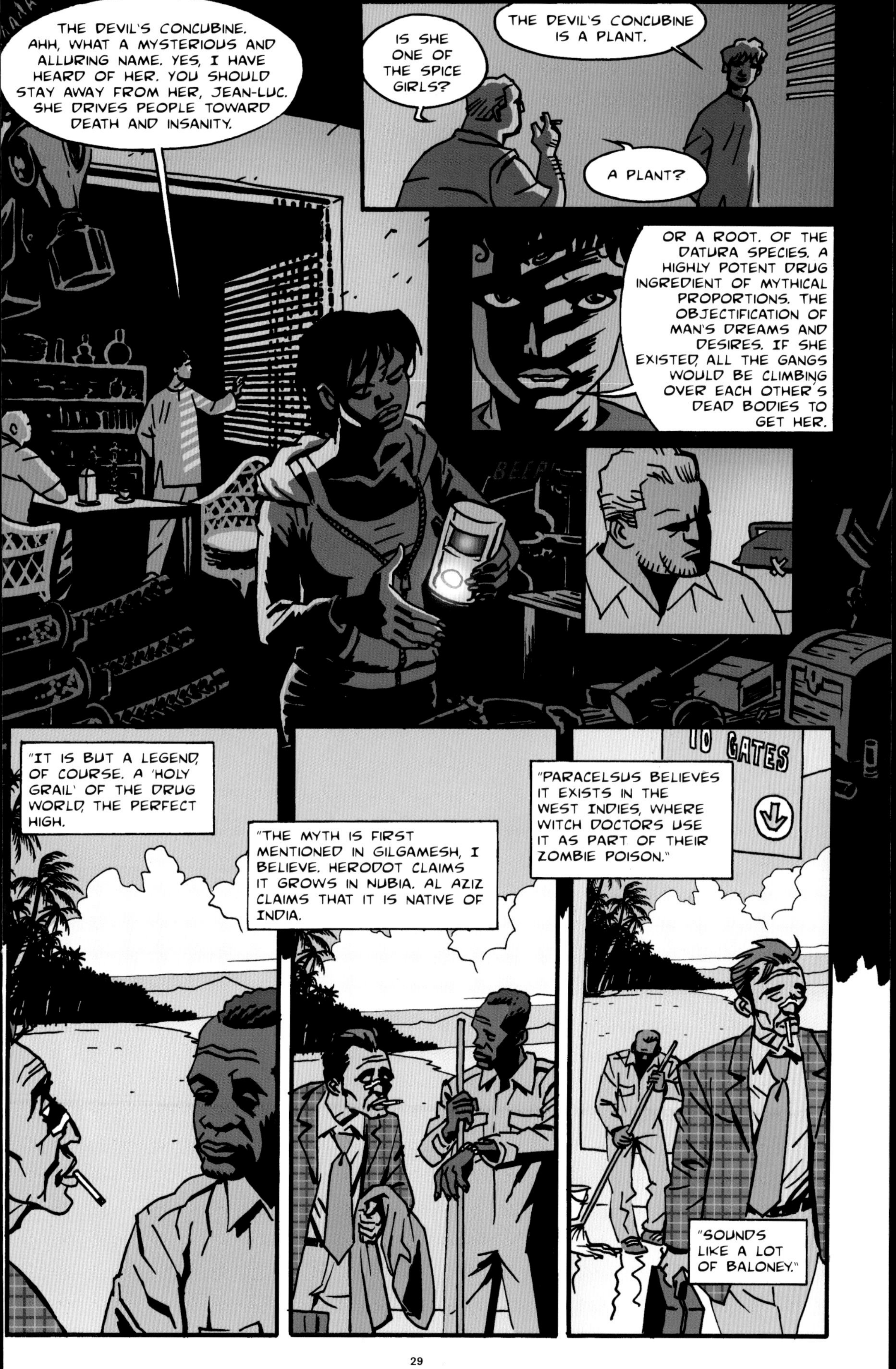
THE DEVIL'S CONCUBINE. AHH, WHAT A MYSTERIOUS AND ALLURING NAME. YES, I HAVE HEARD OF HER. YOU SHOULD STAY AWAY FROM HER, JEAN-LUC. SHE DRIVES PEOPLE TOWARD DEATH AND INSANITY.
IS SHE ONE OF THE SPICE GIRLS?
THE DEVIL'S CONCUBINE IS A PLANT.
A PLANT?
OR A ROOT. OF THE DATURA SPECIES. A HIGHLY POTENT DRUG INGREDIENT OF MYTHICAL PROPORTIONS. THE OBJECTIFICATION OF MAN'S DREAMS AND DESIRES. IF SHE EXISTED, ALL THE GANGS WOULD BE CLIMBING OVER EACH OTHER'S DEAD BODIES TO GET HER.
"IT IS BUT A LEGEND, OF COURSE. A 'HOLY GRAIL' OF THE DRUG WORLD, THE PERFECT HIGH.
"THE MYTH IS FIRST MENTIONED IN GILGAMESH, I BELIEVE. HERODOT CLAIMS IT GROWS IN NUBIA. AL AZIZ CLAIMS THAT IT IS NATIVE OF INDIA.
TO GATES
"PARACELSUS BELIEVES IT EXISTS IN THE WEST INDIES, WHERE WITCH DOCTORS USE IT AS PART OF THEIR ZOMBIE POISON."
"SOUNDS LIKE A LOT OF BALONEY."

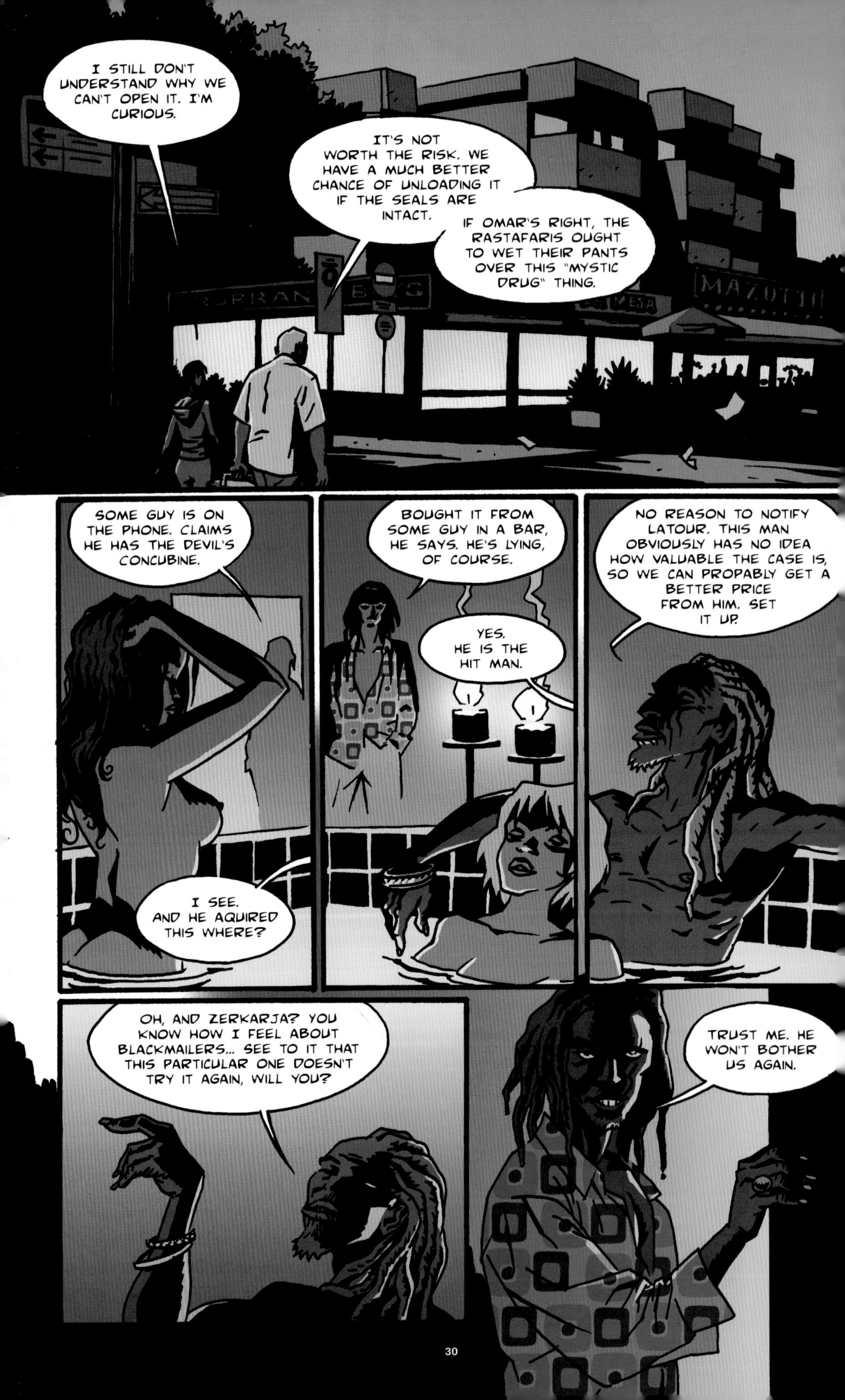
I STILL DON'T UNDERSTAND WHY WE CAN'T OPEN IT. I'M CURIOUS.
IT'S NOT WORTH THE RISK. WE HAVE A MUCH BETTER CHANCE OF UNLOADING IT IF THE SEALS ARE INTACT.
IF OMAR'S RIGHT, THE RASTAFARIS OUGHT TO WET THEIR PANTS OVER THIS "MYSTIC DRUG" THING.
SOME GUY IS ON THE PHONE. CLAIMS HE HAS THE DEVIL'S CONCUBINE.
I SEE. AND HE AQUIRED THIS WHERE?
BOUGHT IT FROM SOME GUY IN A BAR, HE SAYS. HE'S LYING, OF COURSE.
YES. HE IS THE HIT MAN.
NO REASON TO NOTIFY LATOUR. THIS MAN OBVIOUSLY HAS NO IDEA HOW VALUABLE THE CASE IS, SO WE CAN PROPABLY GET A BETTER PRICE FROM HIM. SET IT UP.
OH, AND ZERKARJA? YOU KNOW HOW I FEEL ABOUT BLACKMAILERS... SEE TO IT THAT THIS PARTICULAR ONE DOESN'T TRY IT AGAIN, WILL YOU?
TRUST ME. HE WON'T BOTHER US AGAIN.

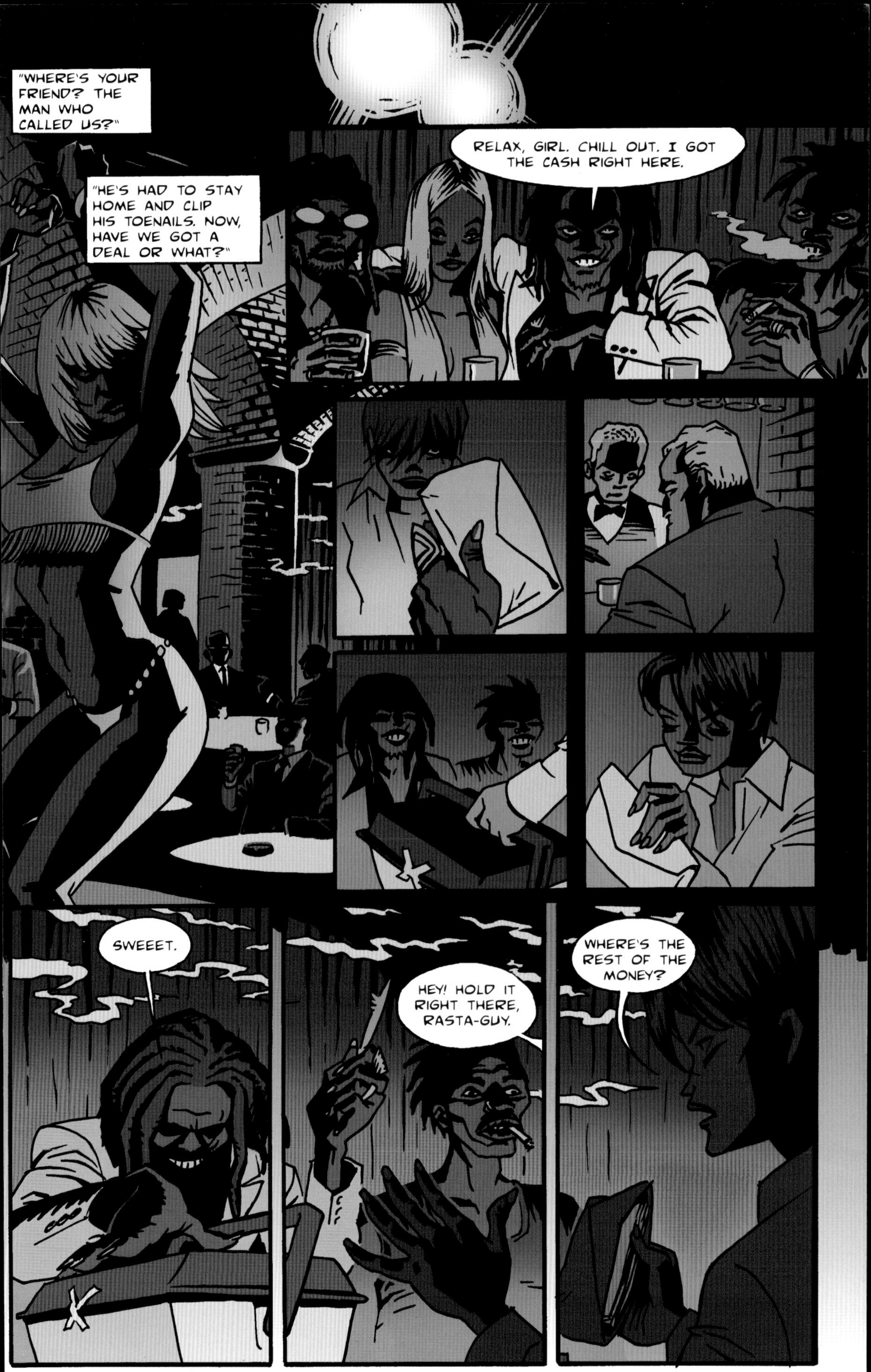
"WHERE'S YOUR FRIEND? THE MAN WHO CALLED US?"
"HE'S HAD TO STAY HOME AND CLIP HIS TOENAILS. NOW, HAVE WE GOT A DEAL OR WHAT?"
RELAX, GIRL. CHILL OUT. I GOT THE CASH RIGHT HERE.
SWEEET.
HEY! HOLD IT RIGHT THERE, RASTA-GUY.
WHERE'S THE REST OF THE MONEY?

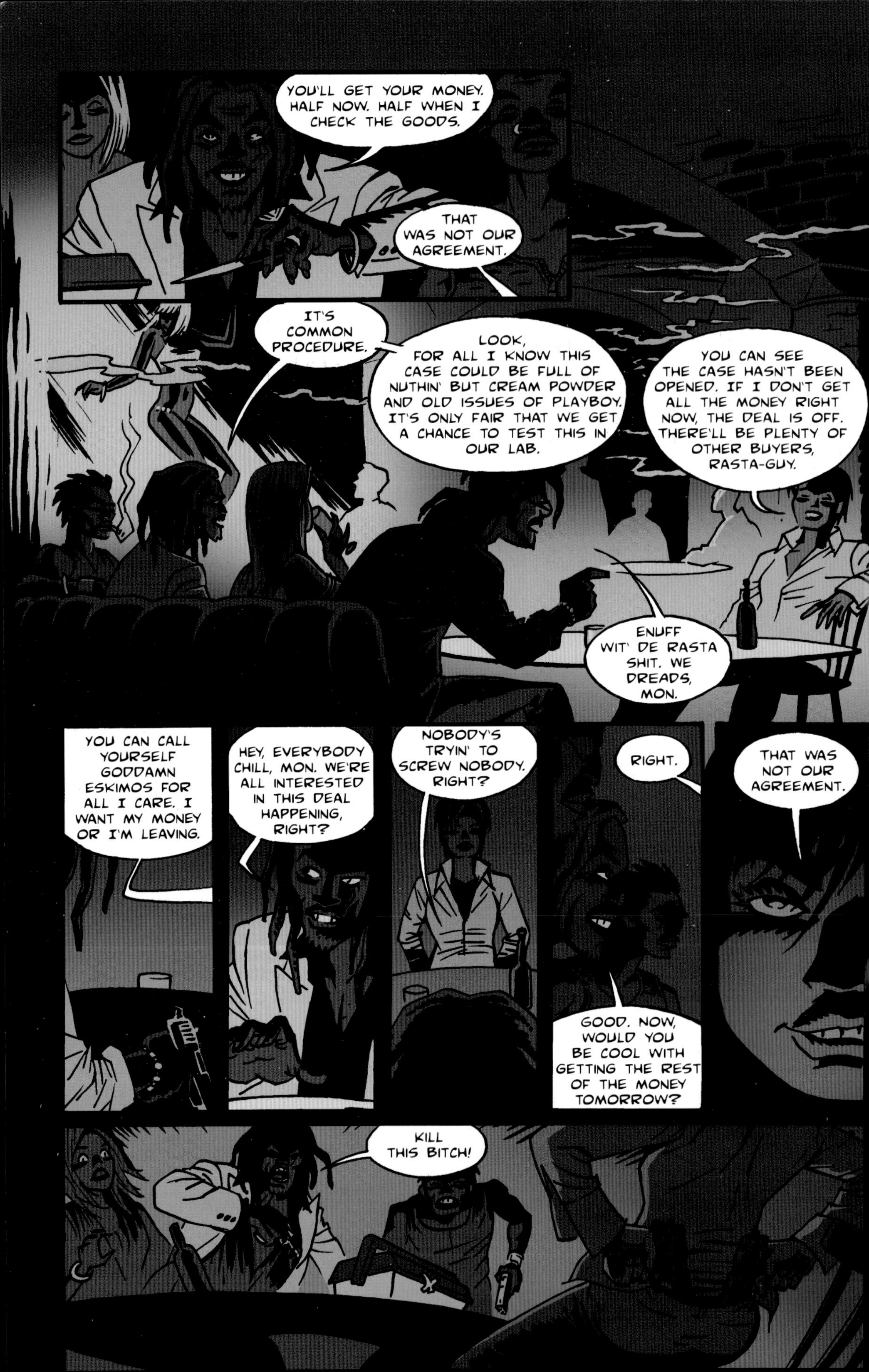

YOU'LL GET YOUR MONEY. HALF NOW. HALF WHEN I CHECK THE GOODS.
THAT WAS NOT OUR AGREEMENT.
IT'S COMMON PROCEDURE.
LOOK, FOR ALL I KNOW THIS CASE COULD BE FULL OF NUTHIN' BUT CREAM POWDER AND OLD ISSUES OF PLAYBOY. IT'S ONLY FAIR THAT WE GET A CHANCE TO TEST THIS IN OUR LAB.
YOU CAN SEE THE CASE HASN'T BEEN OPENED. IF I DON'T GET ALL THE MONEY RIGHT NOW, THE DEAL IS OFF. THERE'LL BE PLENTY OF OTHER BUYERS, RASTA-GUY.
ENUFF WIT' DE RASTA SHIT. WE DREADS, MON.
YOU CAN CALL YOURSELF GODDAMN ESKIMOS FOR ALL I CARE. I WANT MY MONEY OR I'M LEAVING.
HEY, EVERYBODY CHILL, MON. WE'RE ALL INTERESTED IN THIS DEAL HAPPENING, RIGHT?
NOBODY'S TRYIN' TO SCREW NOBODY. RIGHT?
RIGHT.
GOOD. NOW, WOULD YOU BE COOL WITH GETTING THE REST OF THE MONEY TOMORROW?
THAT WAS NOT OUR AGREEMENT.
KILL THIS BITCH!

PART II

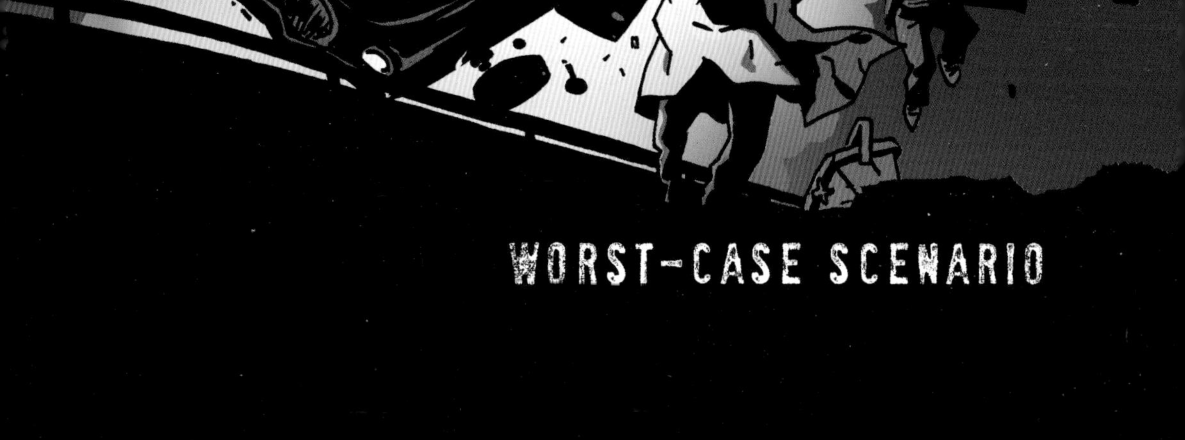

WORST-CASE SCENARIO

"You're one of those the-glass-is-half-empty types, right?"

–*Linda*

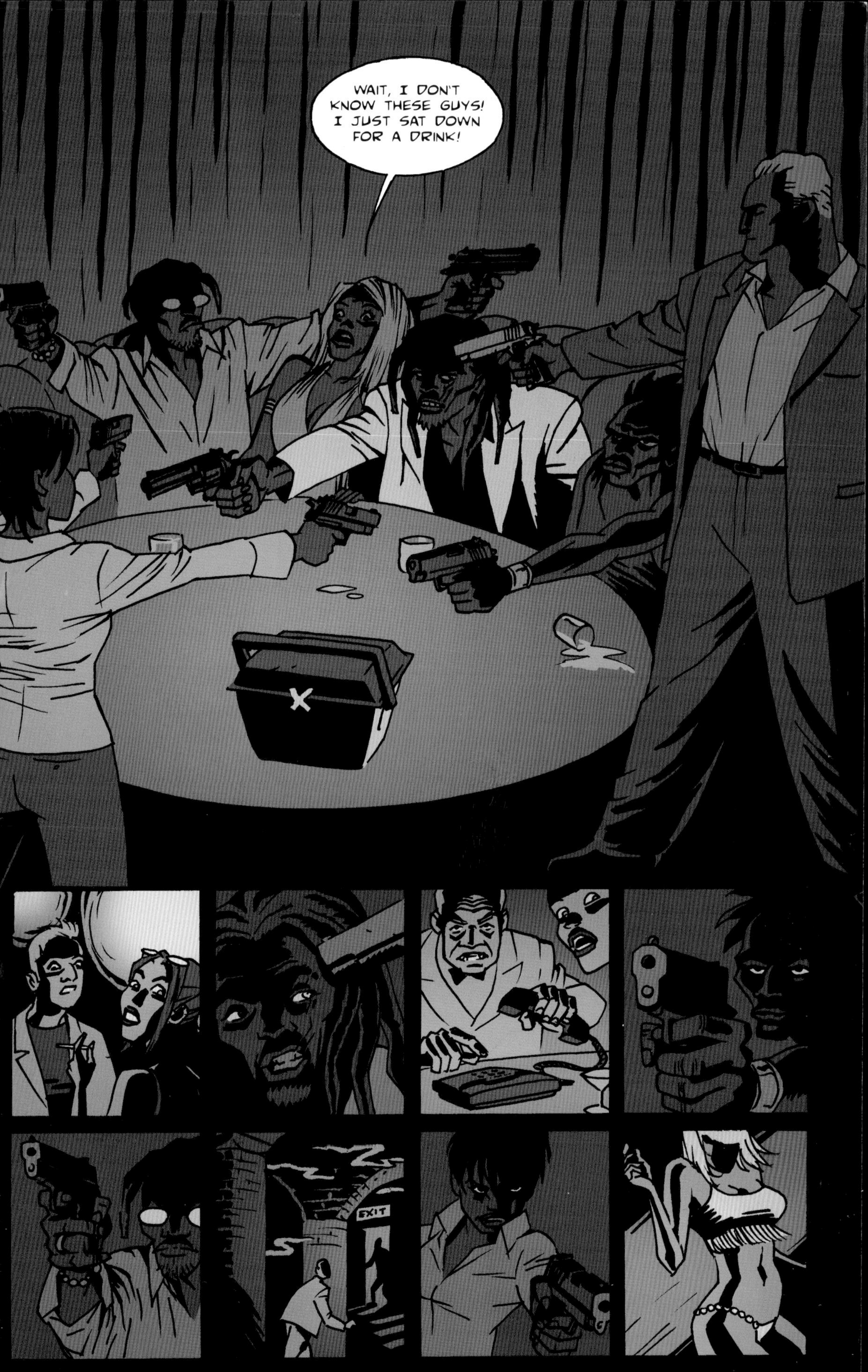
WAIT, I DON'T KNOW THESE GUYS! I JUST SAT DOWN FOR A DRINK!
EXIT

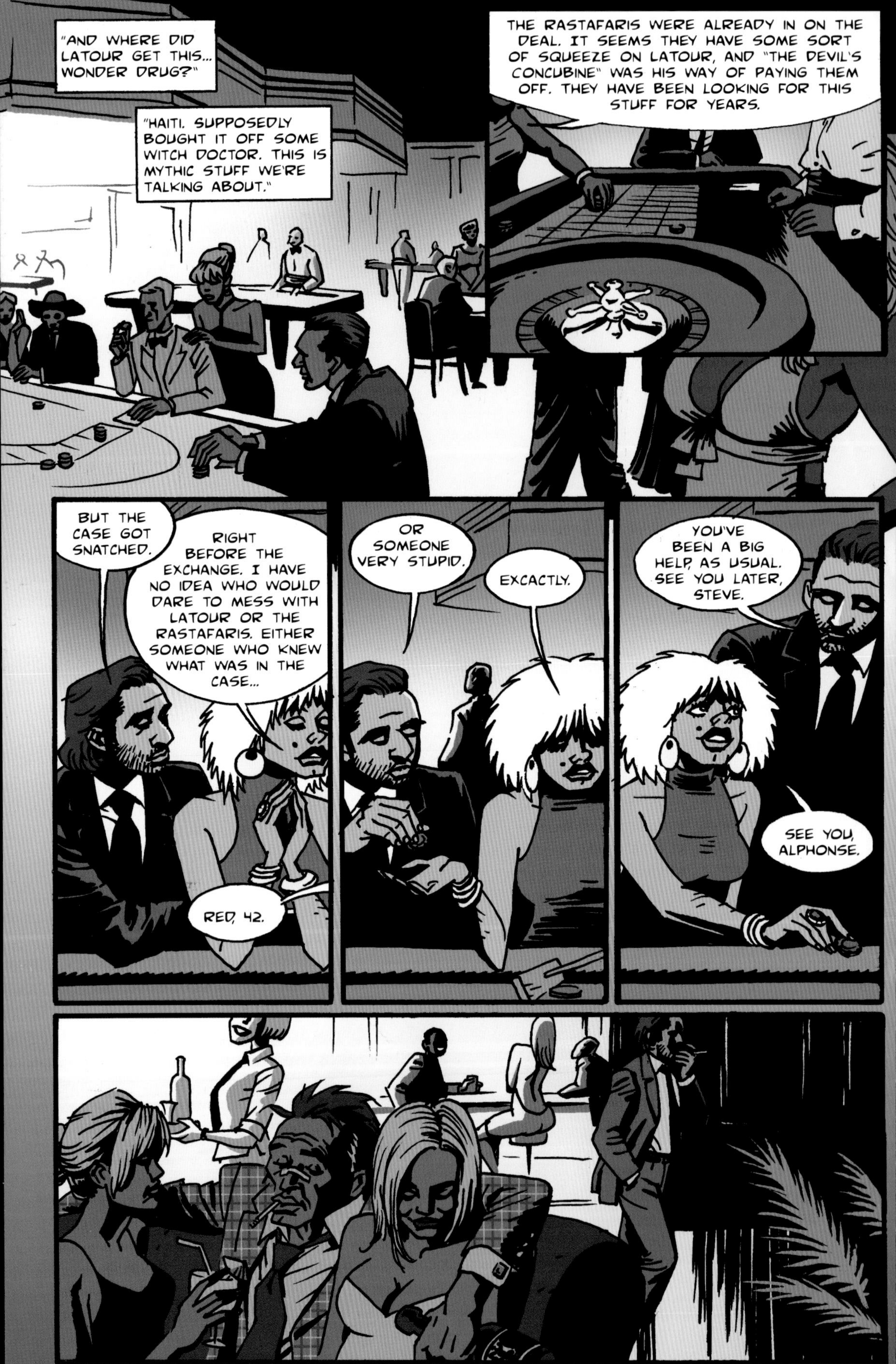
"AND WHERE DID LATOUR GET THIS... WONDER DRUG?"
"HAITI. SUPPOSEDLY BOUGHT IT OFF SOME WITCH DOCTOR. THIS IS MYTHIC STUFF WE'RE TALKING ABOUT."
THE RASTAFARIS WERE ALREADY IN ON THE DEAL. IT SEEMS THEY HAVE SOME SORT OF SQUEEZE ON LATOUR, AND "THE DEVIL'S CONCUBINE" WAS HIS WAY OF PAYING THEM OFF. THEY HAVE BEEN LOOKING FOR THIS STUFF FOR YEARS.
BUT THE CASE GOT SNATCHED.
RIGHT BEFORE THE EXCHANGE. I HAVE NO IDEA WHO WOULD DARE TO MESS WITH LATOUR OR THE RASTAFARIS. EITHER SOMEONE WHO KNEW WHAT WAS IN THE CASE...
RED, 42.
OR SOMEONE VERY STUPID.
EXCACTLY.
YOU'VE BEEN A BIG HELP, AS USUAL. SEE YOU LATER, STEVE.
SEE YOU, ALPHONSE.

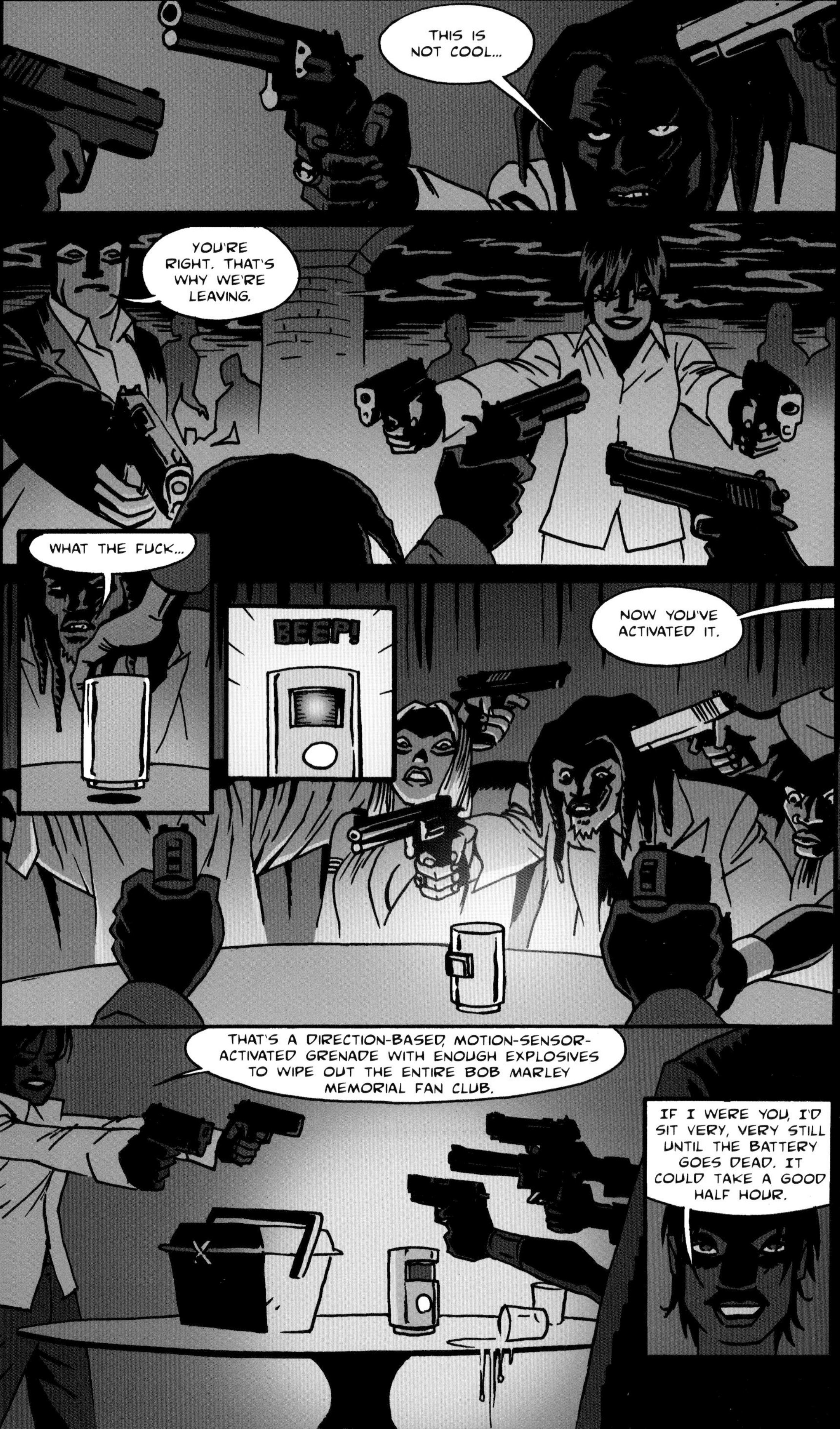
THIS IS NOT COOL...
YOU'RE RIGHT. THAT'S WHY WE'RE LEAVING.
WHAT THE FUCK...
BEEP!
NOW YOU'VE ACTIVATED IT.
THAT'S A DIRECTION-BASED, MOTION-SENSOR-ACTIVATED GRENADE WITH ENOUGH EXPLOSIVES TO WIPE OUT THE ENTIRE BOB MARLEY MEMORIAL FAN CLUB.
IF I WERE YOU, I'D SIT VERY, VERY STILL UNTIL THE BATTERY GOES DEAD. IT COULD TAKE A GOOD HALF HOUR.

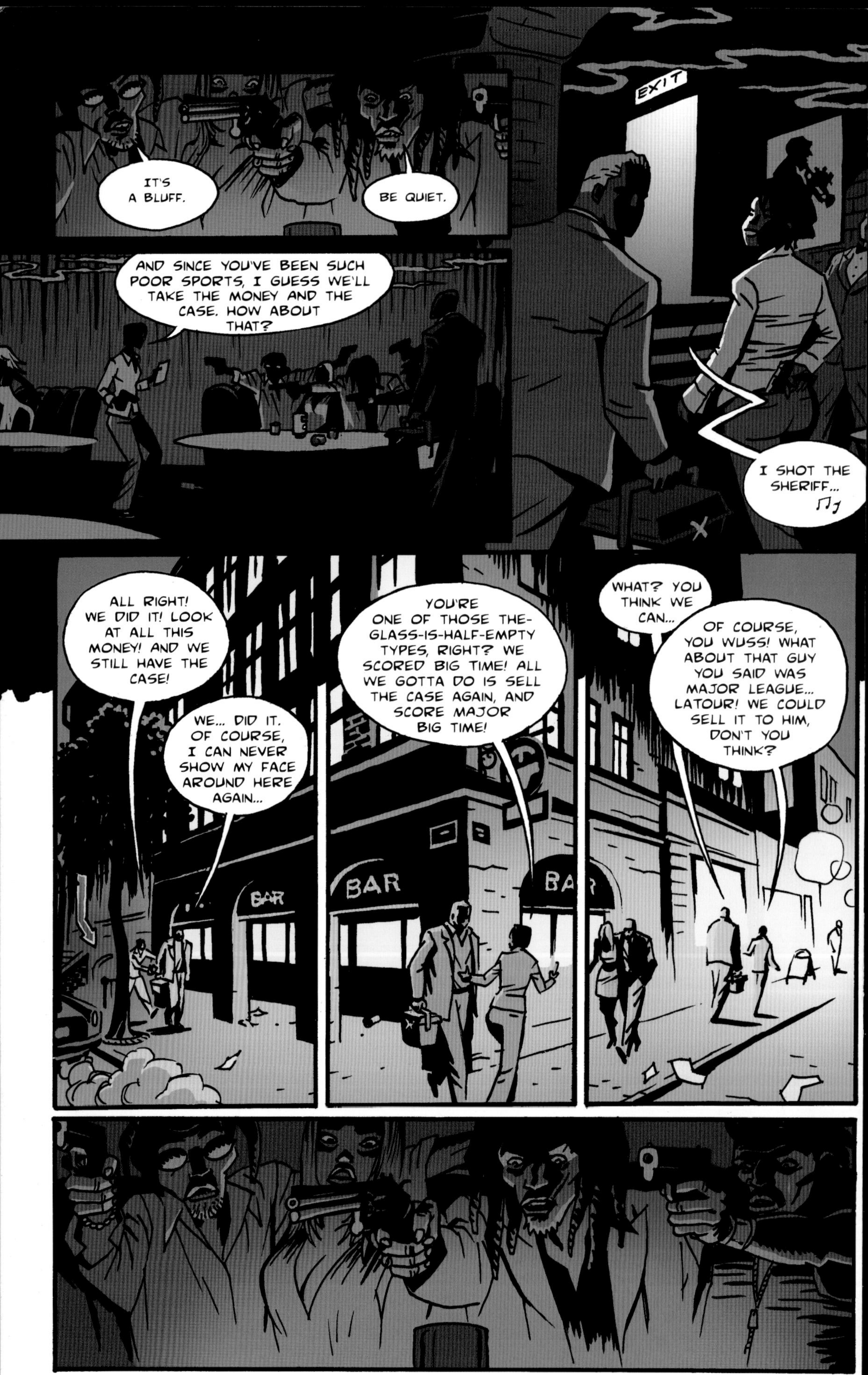
IT'S A BLUFF.
BE QUIET.
AND SINCE YOU'VE BEEN SUCH POOR SPORTS, I GUESS WE'LL TAKE THE MONEY AND THE CASE. HOW ABOUT THAT?
EXIT
I SHOT THE SHERIFF...
ALL RIGHT! WE DID IT! LOOK AT ALL THIS MONEY! AND WE STILL HAVE THE CASE!
WE... DID IT. OF COURSE, I CAN NEVER SHOW MY FACE AROUND HERE AGAIN...
BAR
YOU'RE ONE OF THOSE THE-GLASS-IS-HALF-EMPTY TYPES, RIGHT? WE SCORED BIG TIME! ALL WE GOTTA DO IS SELL THE CASE AGAIN, AND SCORE MAJOR BIG TIME!
BAR
WHAT? YOU THINK WE CAN...
OF COURSE, YOU WUSS! WHAT ABOUT THAT GUY YOU SAID WAS MAJOR LEAGUE... LATOUR! WE COULD SELL IT TO HIM, DON'T YOU THINK?

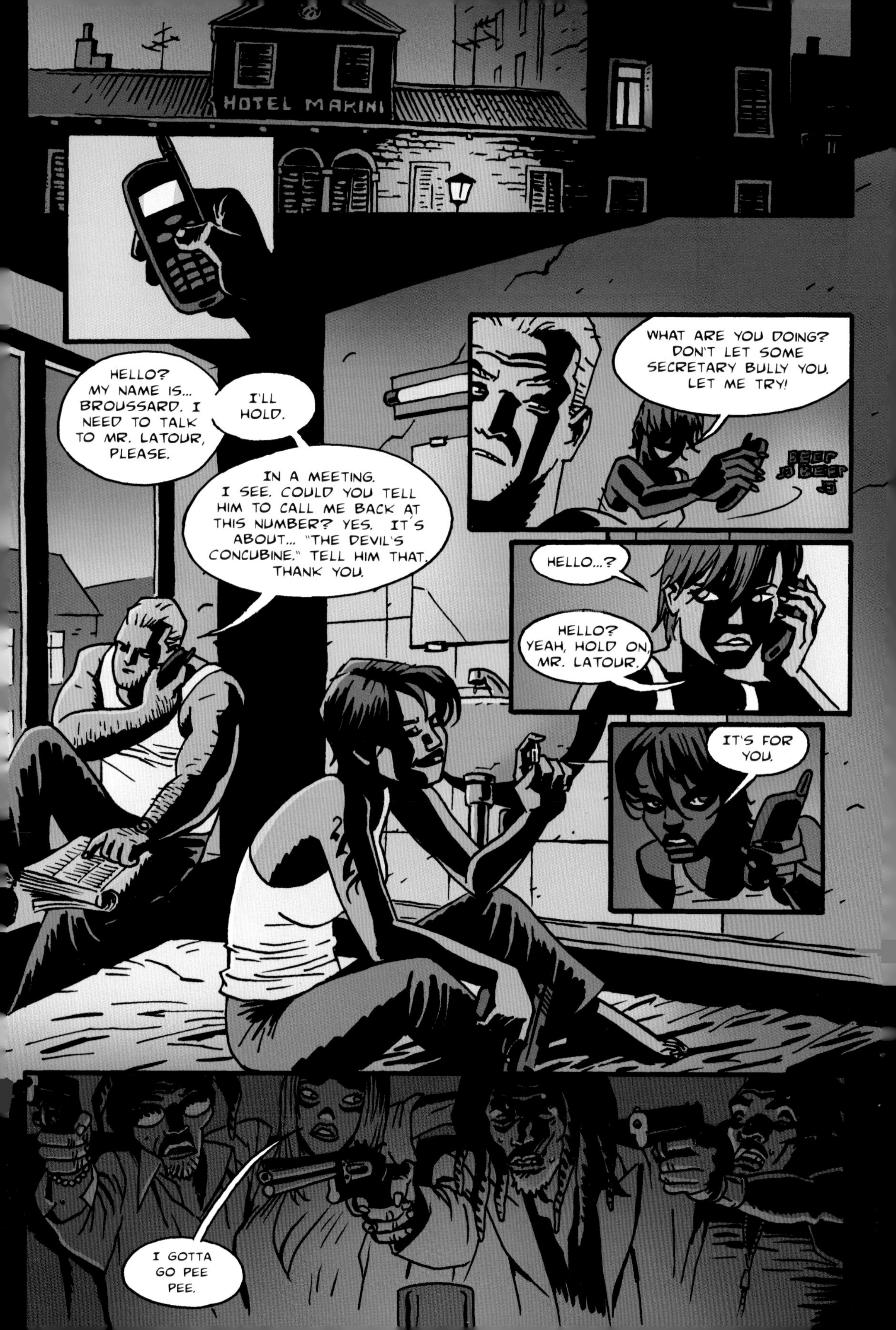
HOTEL MARINI
HELLO? MY NAME IS... BROUSSARD. I NEED TO TALK TO MR. LATOUR, PLEASE.
I'LL HOLD.
IN A MEETING. I SEE. COULD YOU TELL HIM TO CALL ME BACK AT THIS NUMBER? YES. IT'S ABOUT... "THE DEVIL'S CONCUBINE." TELL HIM THAT. THANK YOU.
WHAT ARE YOU DOING? DON'T LET SOME SECRETARY BULLY YOU. LET ME TRY!
BEEP BEEP
HELLO...?
HELLO? YEAH, HOLD ON, MR. LATOUR.
IT'S FOR YOU.
I GOTTA GO PEE PEE.

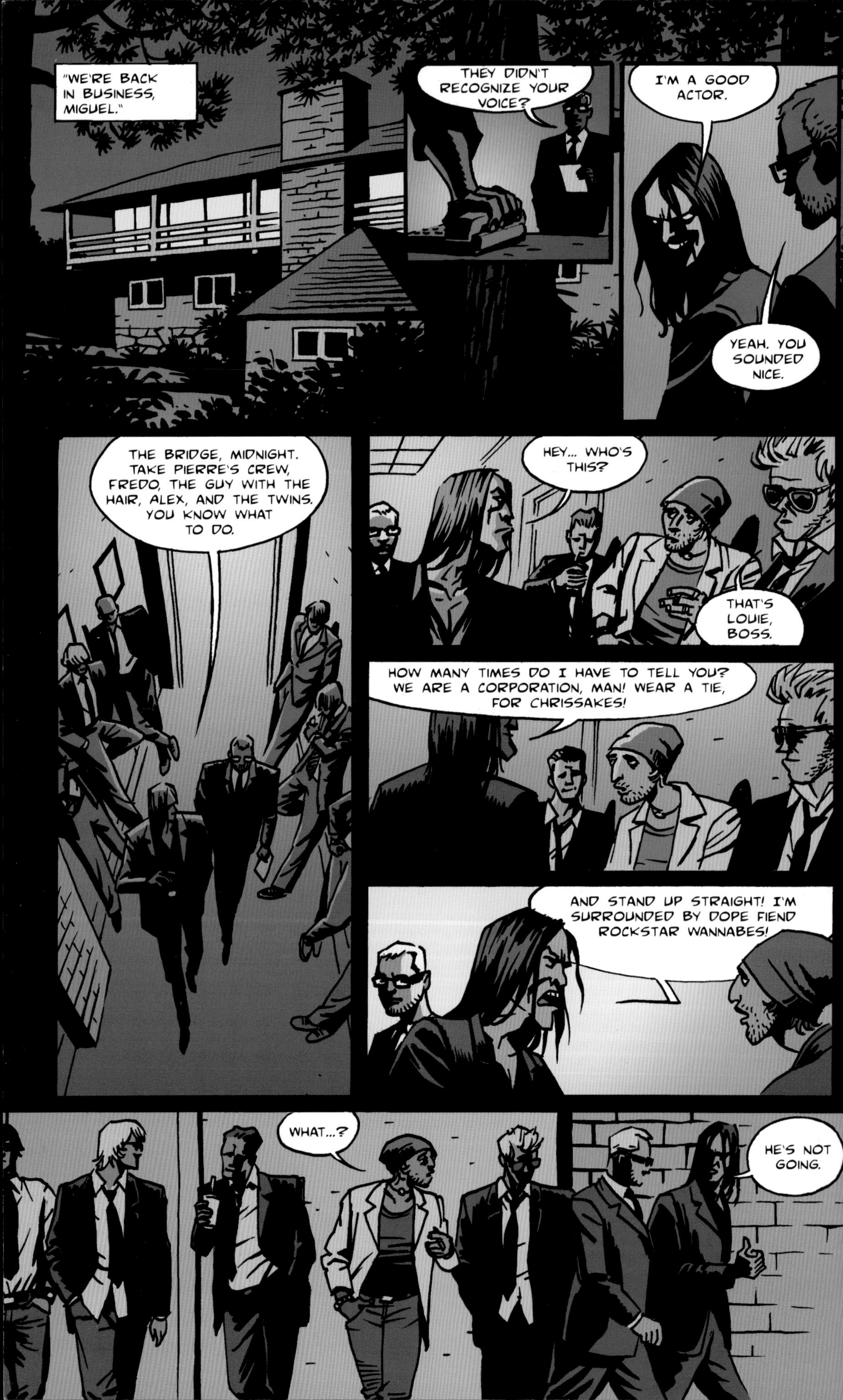
"WE'RE BACK IN BUSINESS, MIGUEL."
THEY DIDN'T RECOGNIZE YOUR VOICE?
I'M A GOOD ACTOR.
YEAH. YOU SOUNDED NICE.
THE BRIDGE, MIDNIGHT. TAKE PIERRE'S CREW, FREDO, THE GUY WITH THE HAIR, ALEX, AND THE TWINS. YOU KNOW WHAT TO DO.
HEY... WHO'S THIS?
THAT'S LOUIE, BOSS.
HOW MANY TIMES DO I HAVE TO TELL YOU? WE ARE A CORPORATION, MAN! WEAR A TIE, FOR CHRISSAKES!
AND STAND UP STRAIGHT! I'M SURROUNDED BY DOPE FIEND ROCKSTAR WANNABES!
WHAT...?
HE'S NOT GOING.

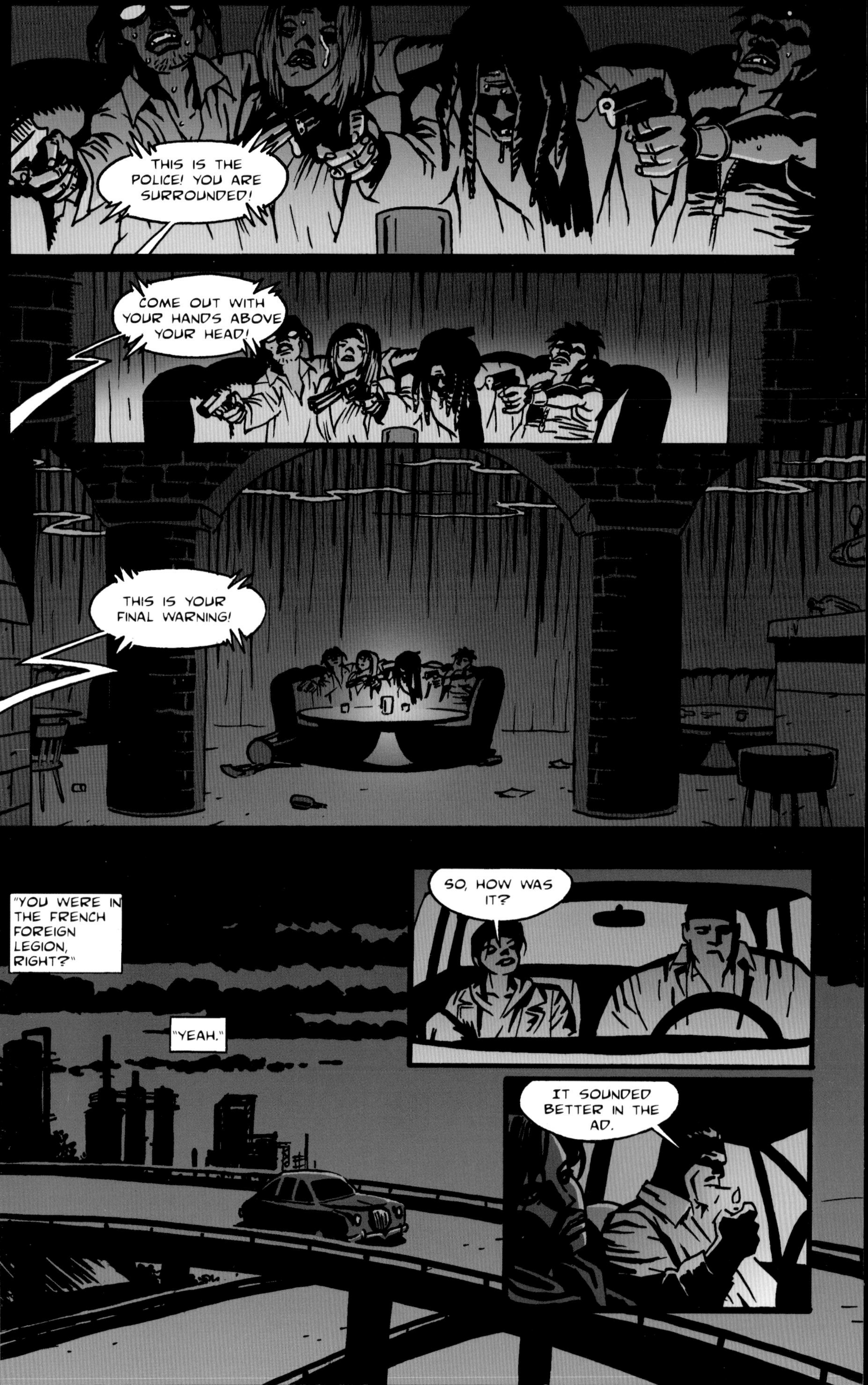
THIS IS THE POLICE! YOU ARE SURROUNDED!
COME OUT WITH YOUR HANDS ABOVE YOUR HEAD!
THIS IS YOUR FINAL WARNING!
"YOU WERE IN THE FRENCH FOREIGN LEGION, RIGHT?"
SO, HOW WAS IT?
"YEAH."
IT SOUNDED BETTER IN THE AD.

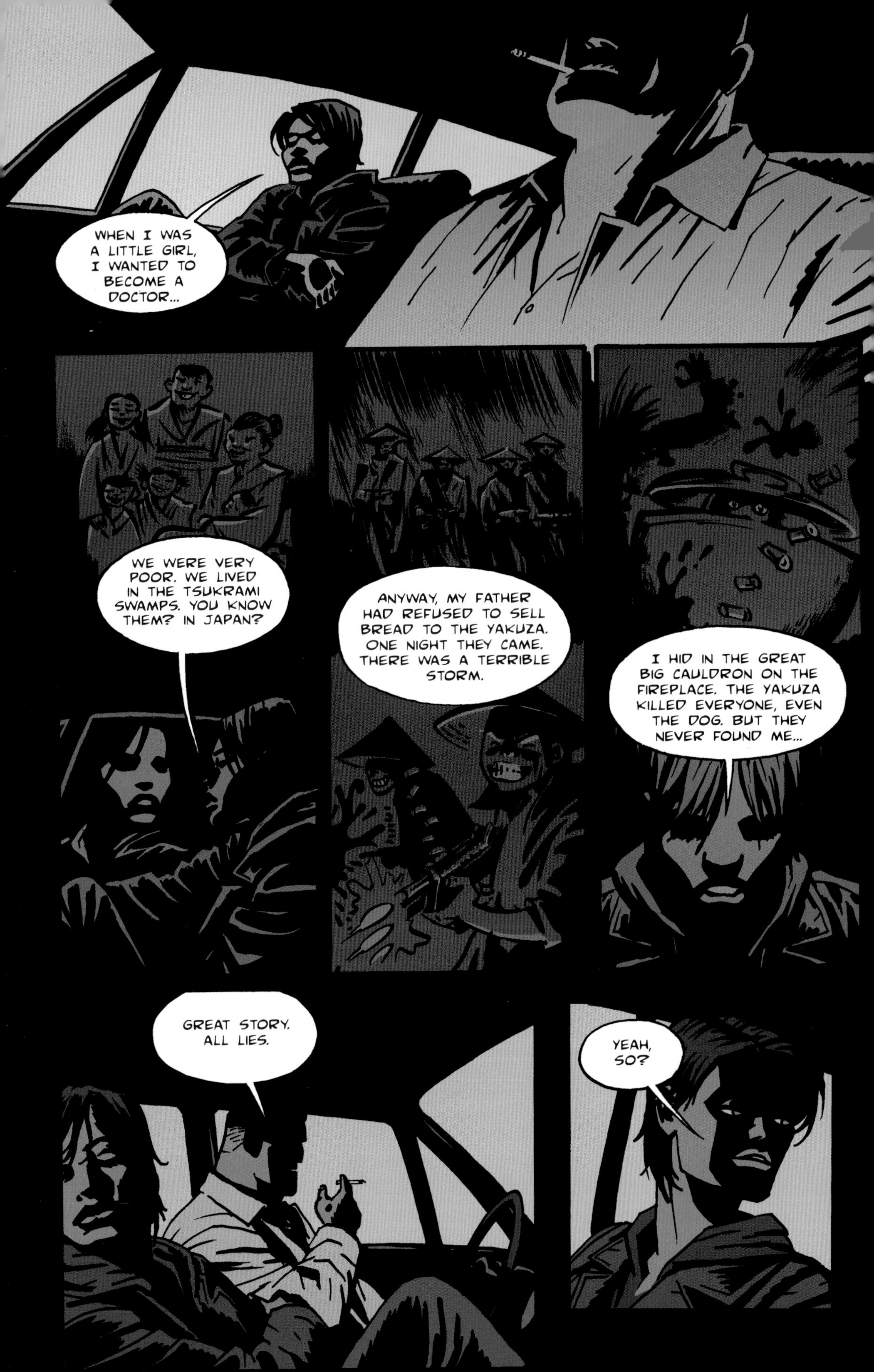
WHEN I WAS A LITTLE GIRL, I WANTED TO BECOME A DOCTOR...
WE WERE VERY POOR. WE LIVED IN THE TSUKRAMI SWAMPS. YOU KNOW THEM? IN JAPAN?
ANYWAY, MY FATHER HAD REFUSED TO SELL BREAD TO THE YAKUZA. ONE NIGHT THEY CAME. THERE WAS A TERRIBLE STORM.
I HID IN THE GREAT BIG CAULDRON ON THE FIREPLACE. THE YAKUZA KILLED EVERYONE, EVEN THE DOG. BUT THEY NEVER FOUND ME...
GREAT STORY. ALL LIES.
YEAH, SO?

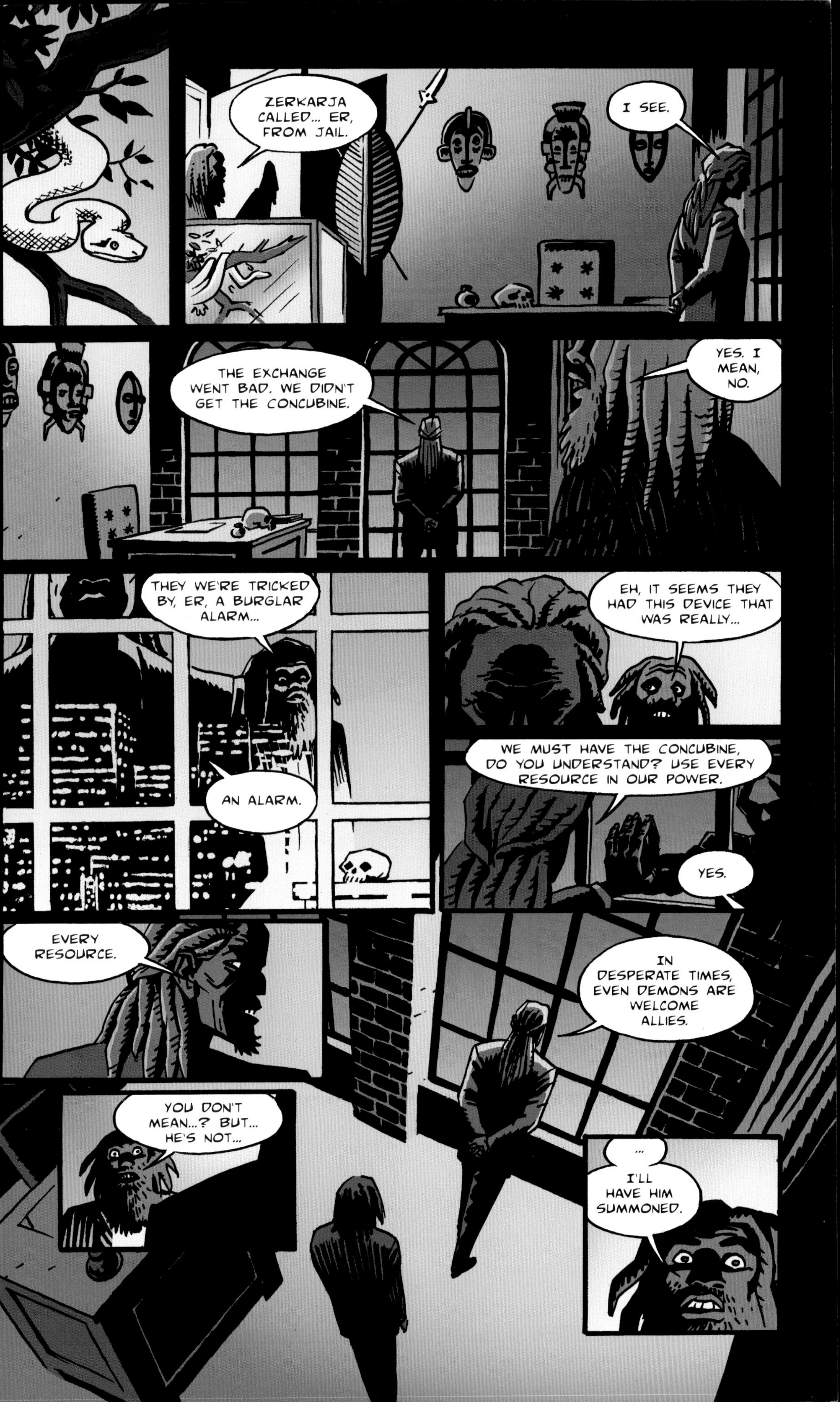
ZERKARJA CALLED... ER, FROM JAIL.
I SEE.
THE EXCHANGE WENT BAD. WE DIDN'T GET THE CONCUBINE.
YES. I MEAN, NO.
THEY WE'RE TRICKED BY, ER, A BURGLAR ALARM...
AN ALARM.
EH, IT SEEMS THEY HAD THIS DEVICE THAT WAS REALLY...
WE MUST HAVE THE CONCUBINE, DO YOU UNDERSTAND? USE EVERY RESOURCE IN OUR POWER.
YES.
EVERY RESOURCE.
IN DESPERATE TIMES, EVEN DEMONS ARE WELCOME ALLIES.
YOU DON'T MEAN...? BUT... HE'S NOT...
...
I'LL HAVE HIM SUMMONED.

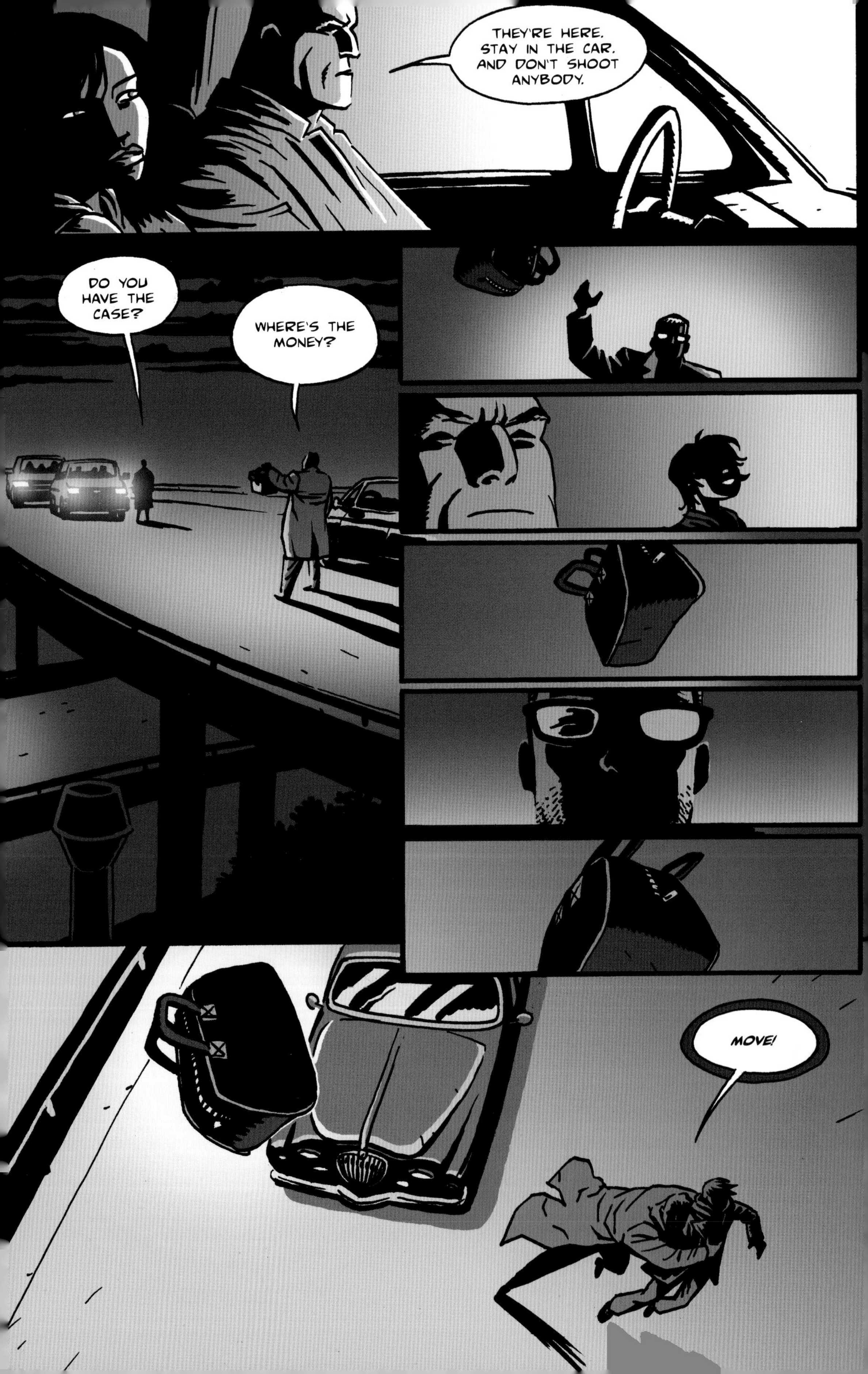
THEY'RE HERE. STAY IN THE CAR. AND DON'T SHOOT ANYBODY.
DO YOU HAVE THE CASE?
WHERE'S THE MONEY?
MOVE!

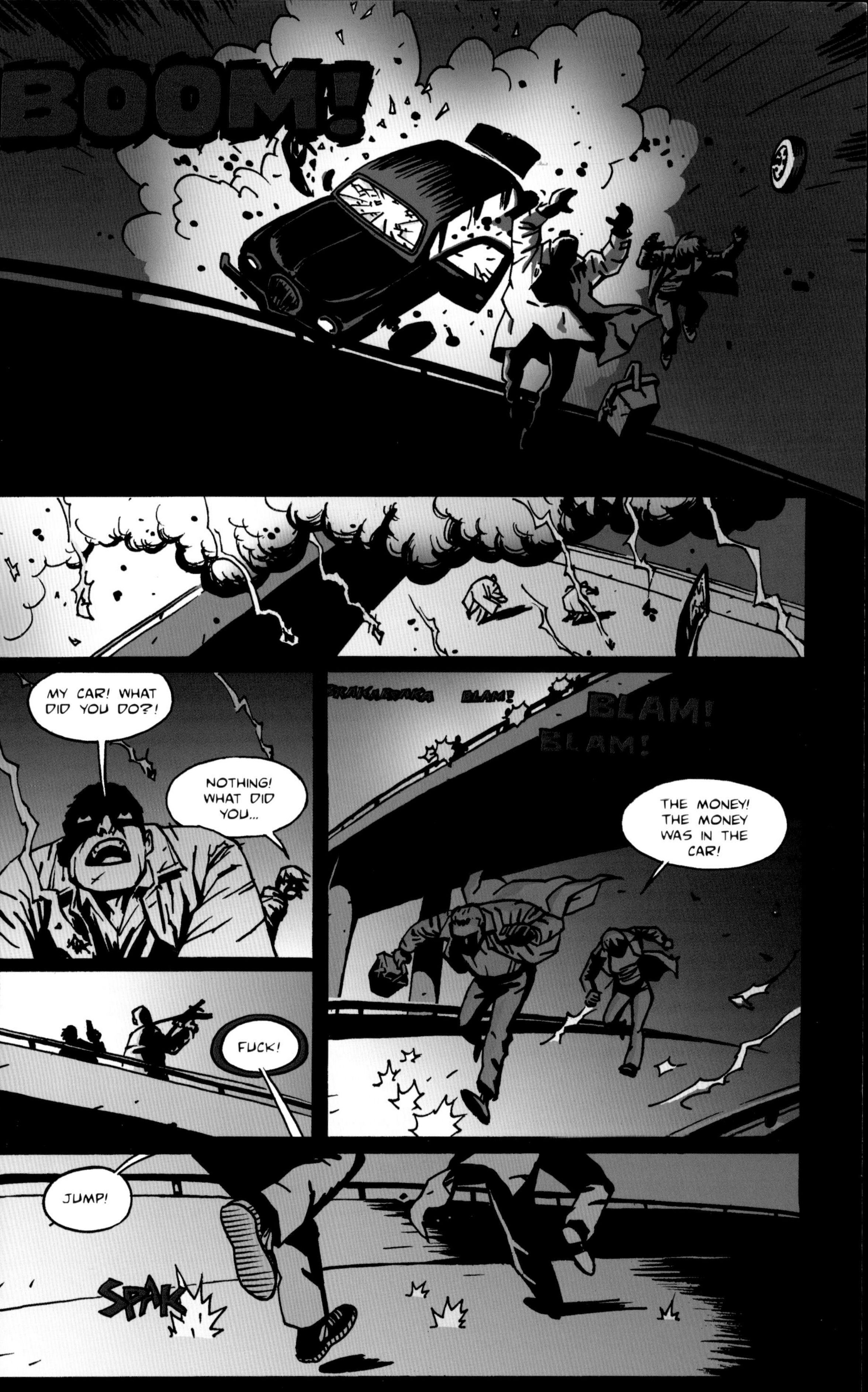
BOOM!
MY CAR! WHAT DID YOU DO?!
NOTHING! WHAT DID YOU...
BLAM!
BLAM!
BLAM!
THE MONEY! THE MONEY WAS IN THE CAR!
FUCK!
JUMP!
SPAK

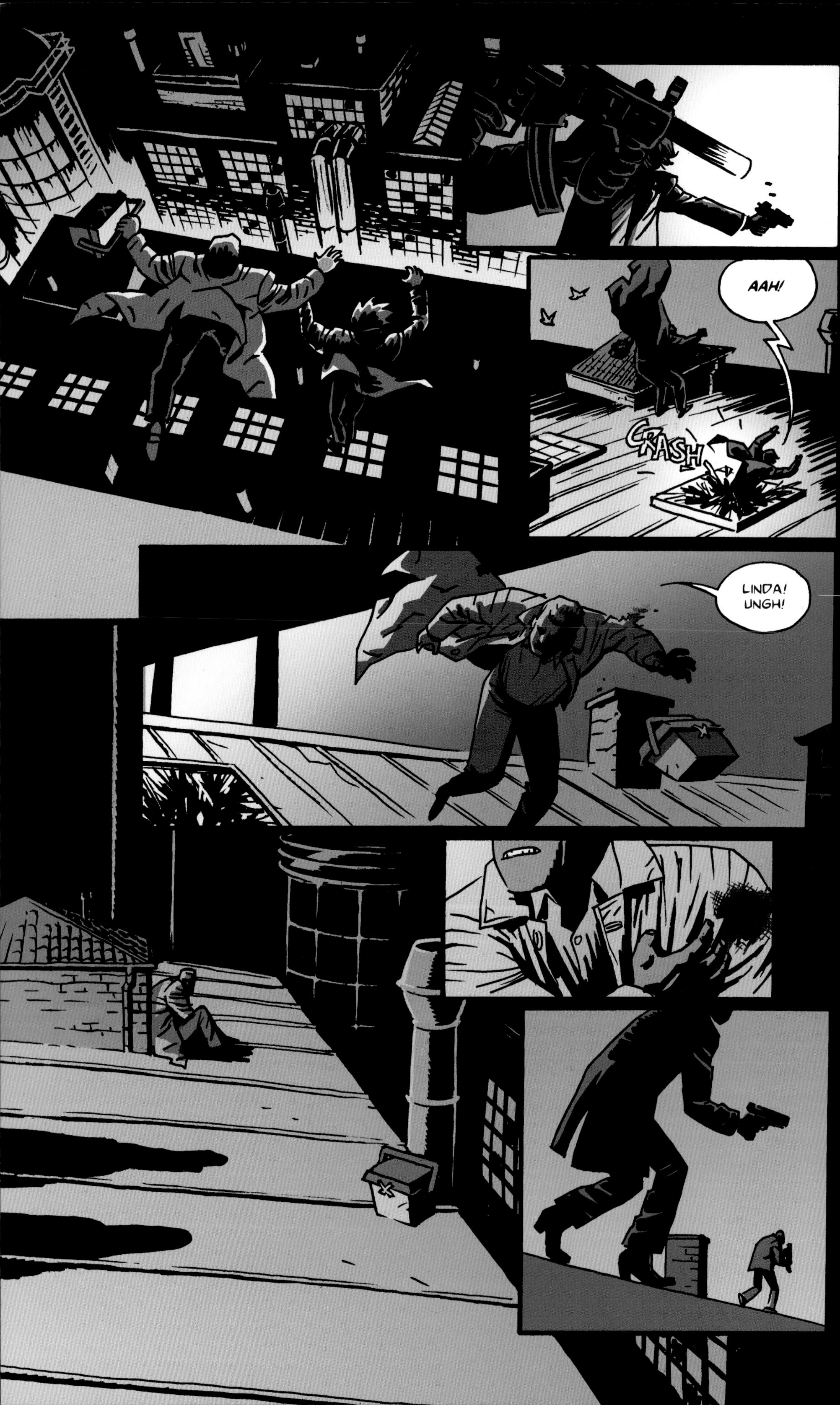
AAH!
CRASH
LINDA! UNGH!

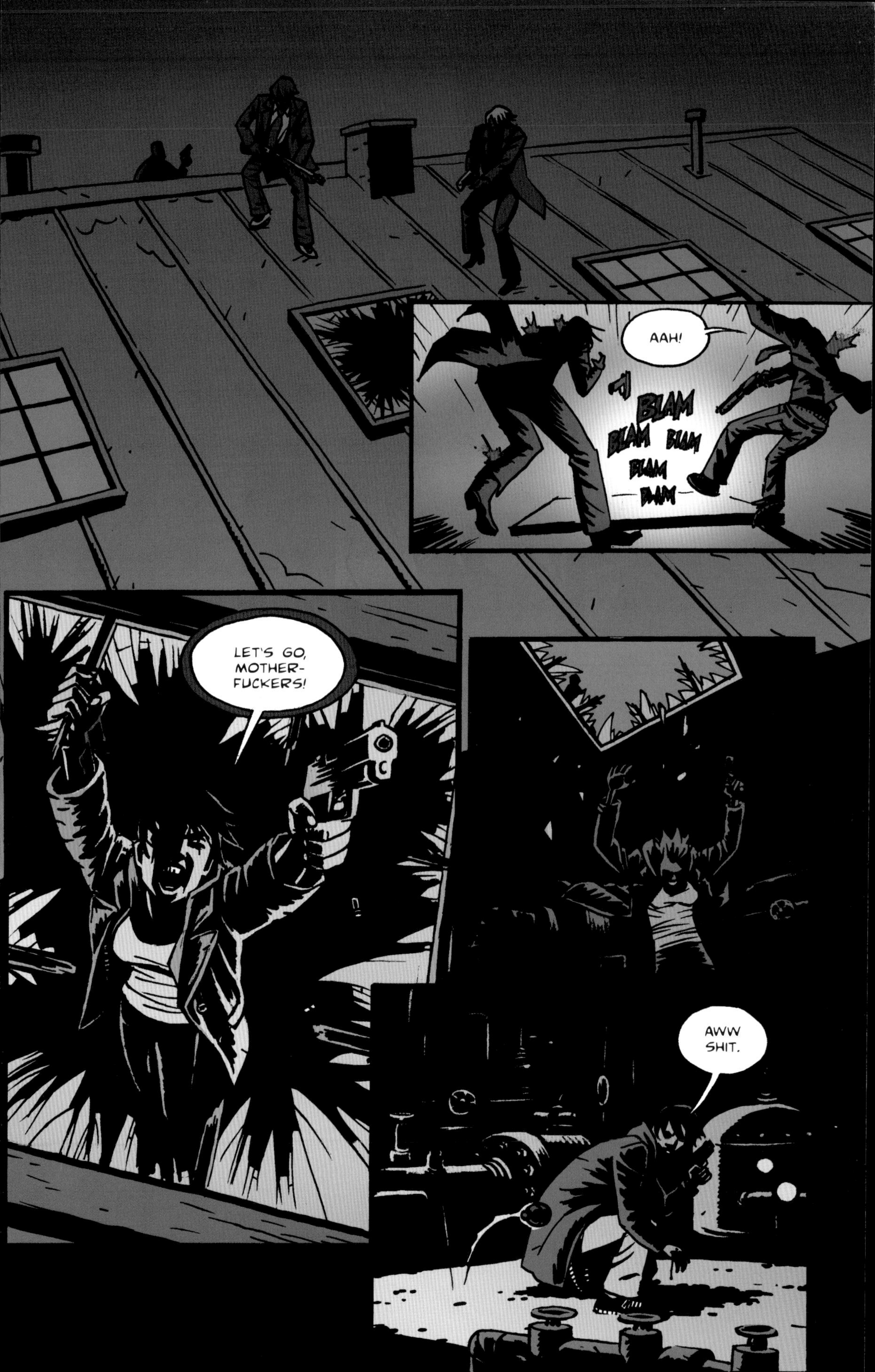
AAH!
BLAM
BLAM BLAM
BLAM
BLAM
LET'S GO, MOTHER-FUCKERS!
AWW SHIT.

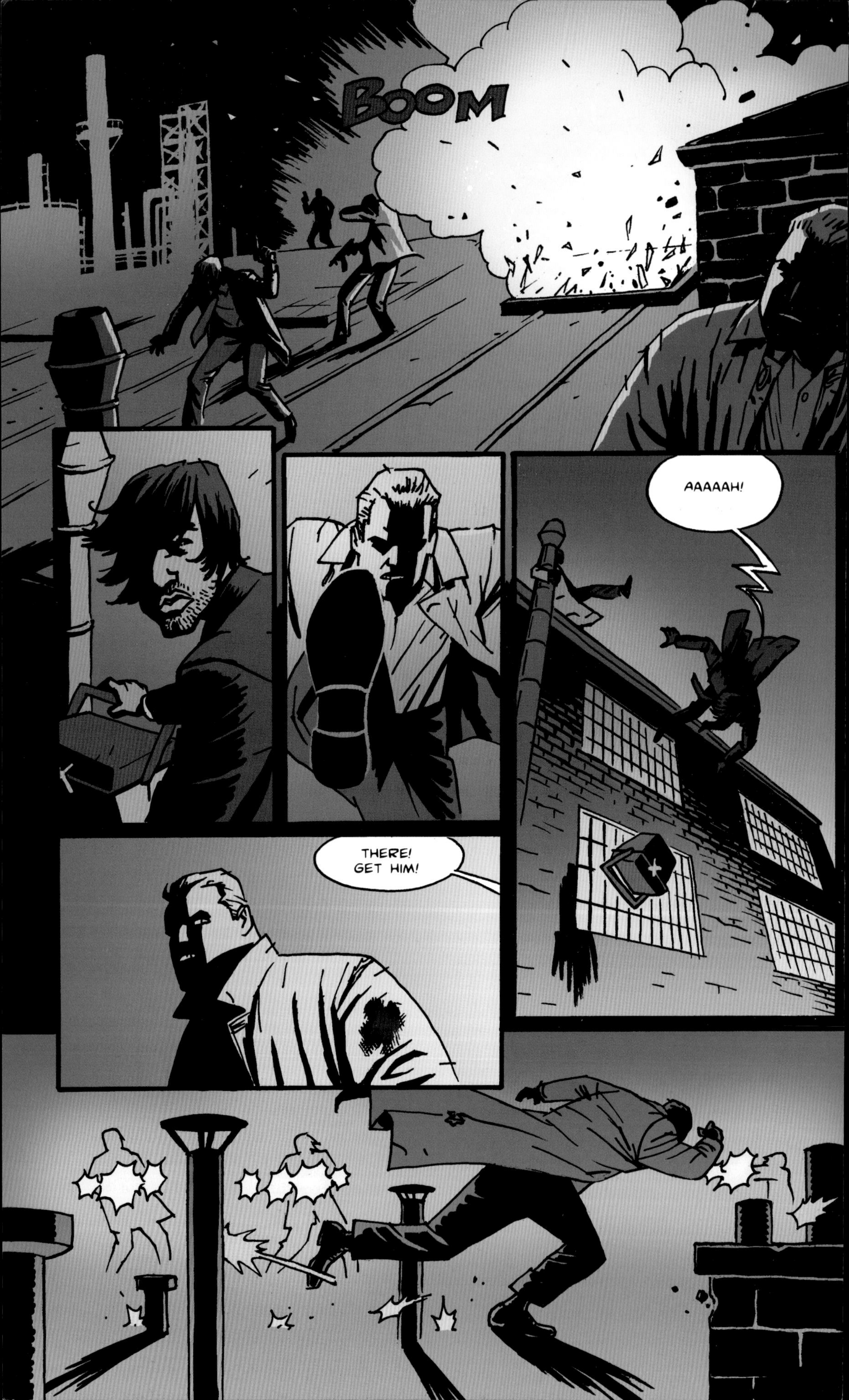
BOOM
AAAAAH!
THERE! GET HIM!

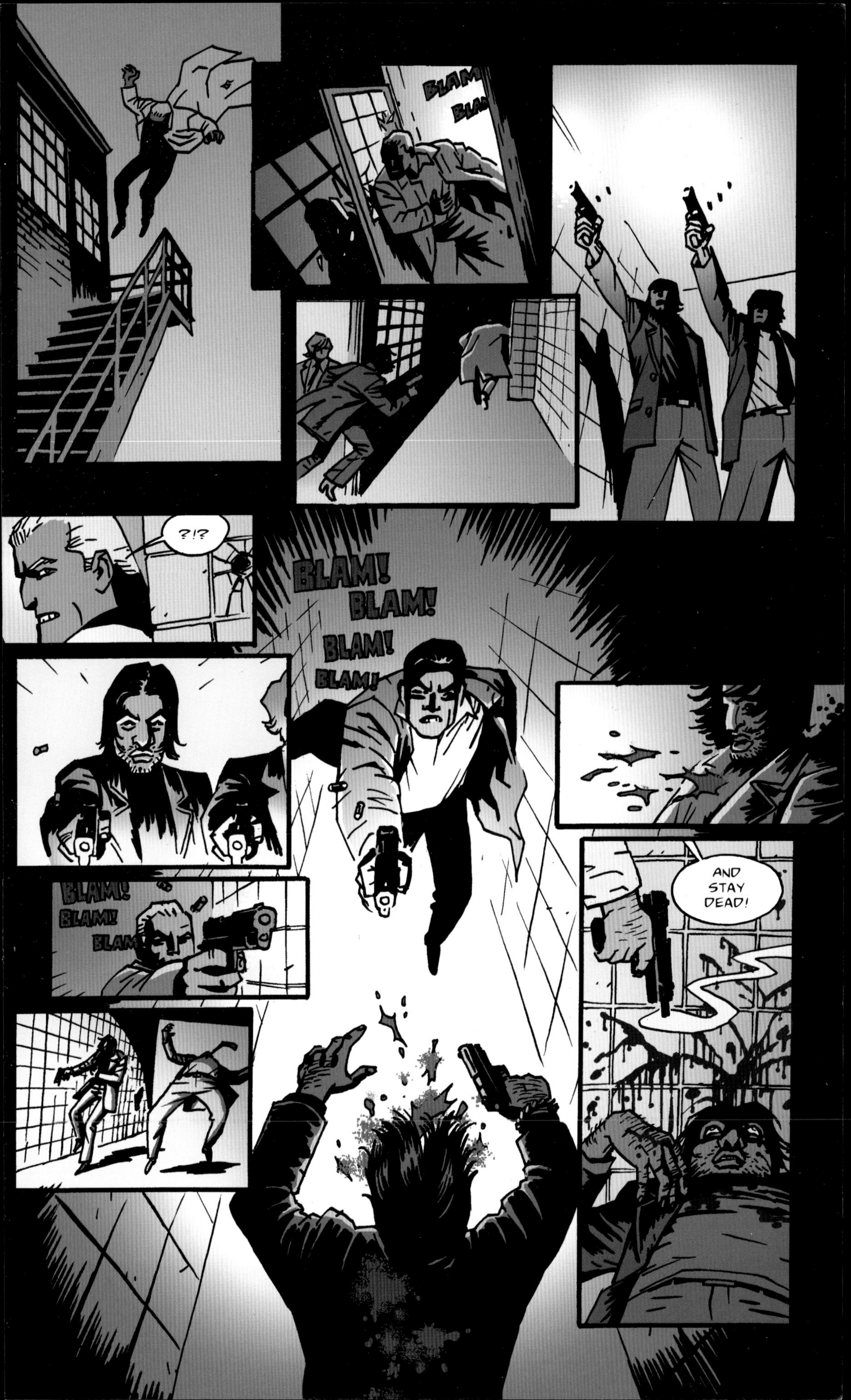
BLAM!
BLAM!
?!?
BLAM!
BLAM!
BLAM!
BLAM!
BLAM!
BLAM!
AND STAY DEAD!

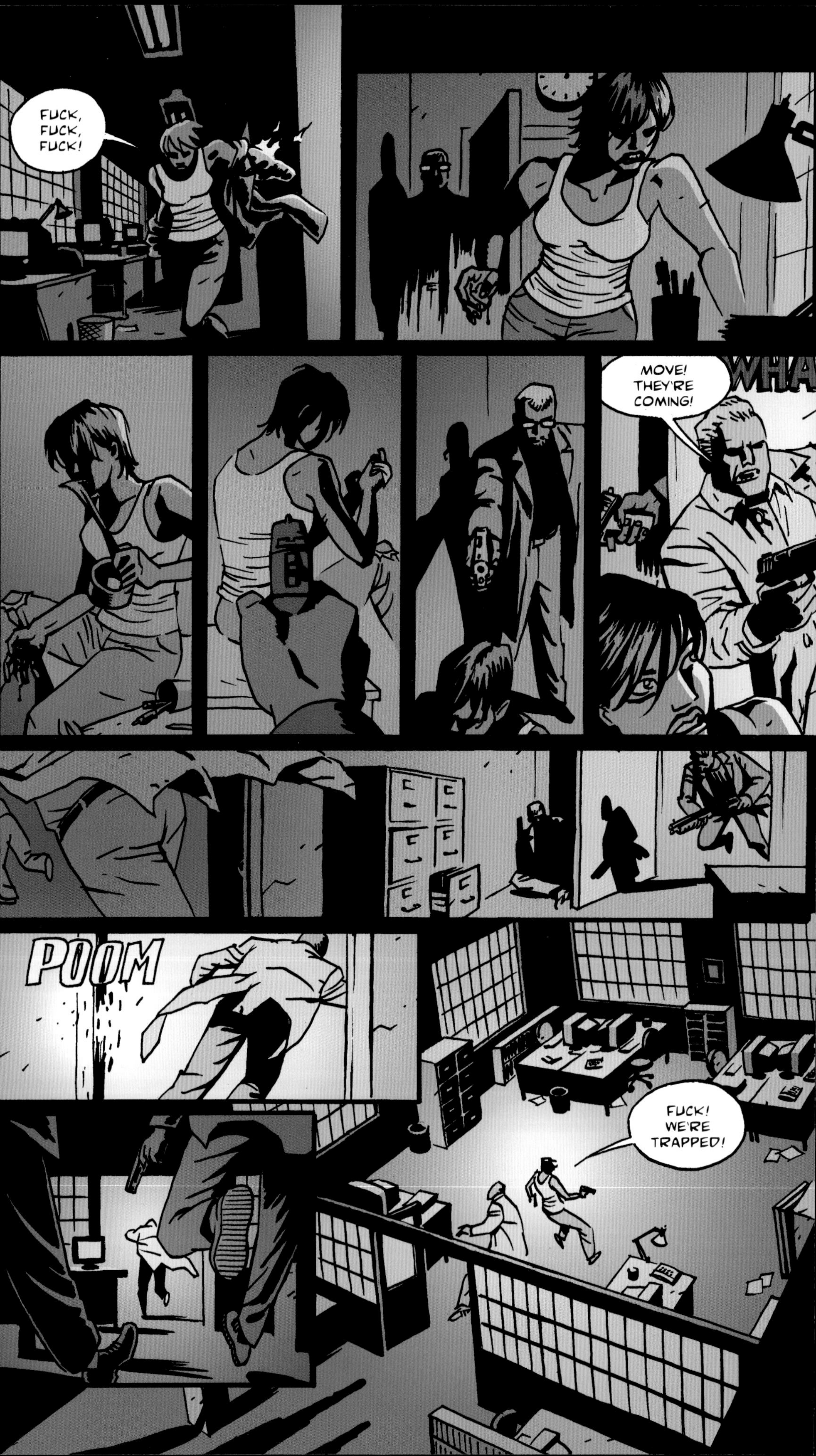
FUCK,
FUCK,
FUCK!
MOVE!
THEY'RE
COMING!
POOM
FUCK!
WE'RE
TRAPPED!

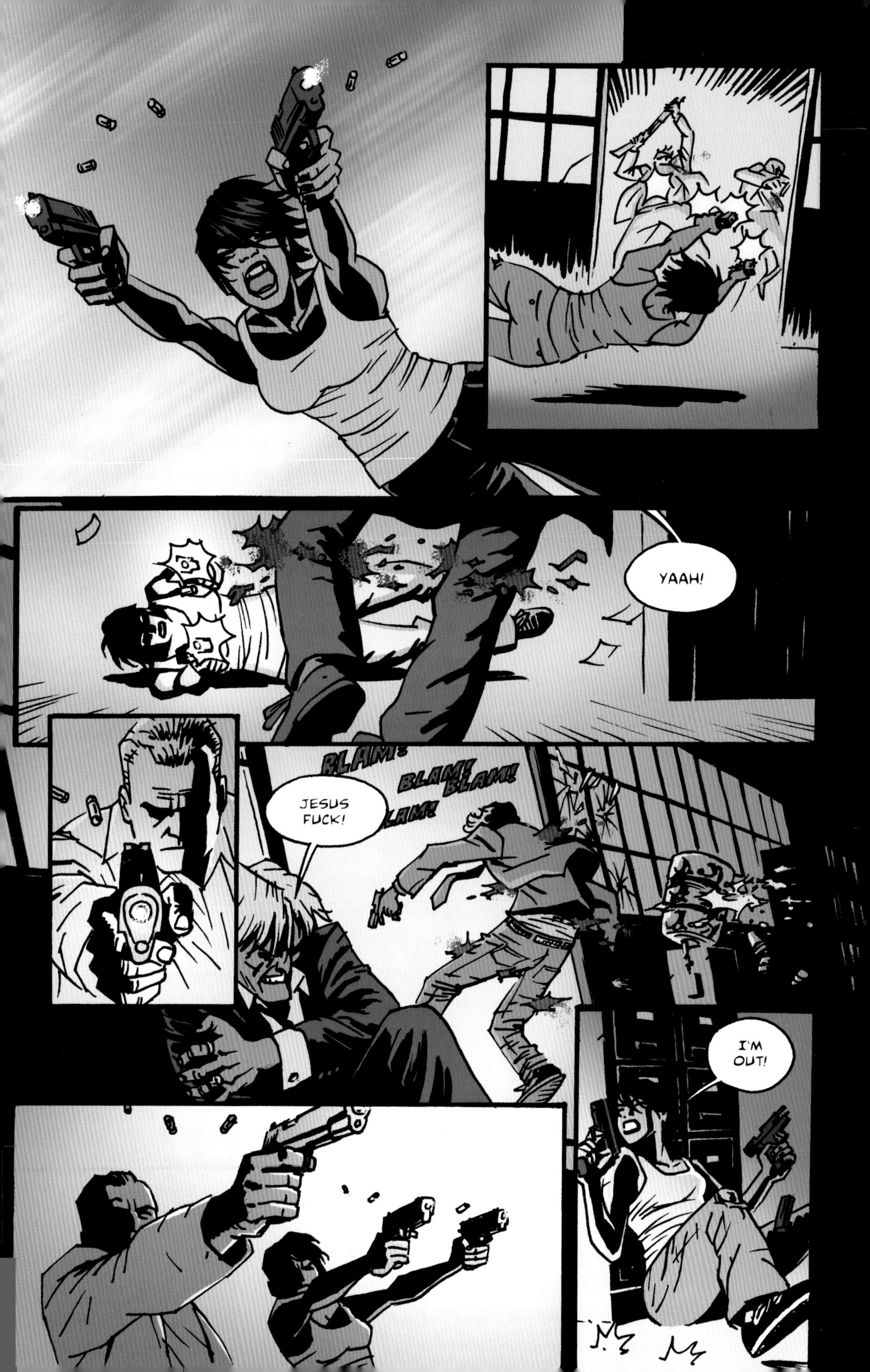
YAAH!
JESUS FUCK!
BLAM!
BLAM! BLAM!
LAM!
I'M OUT!

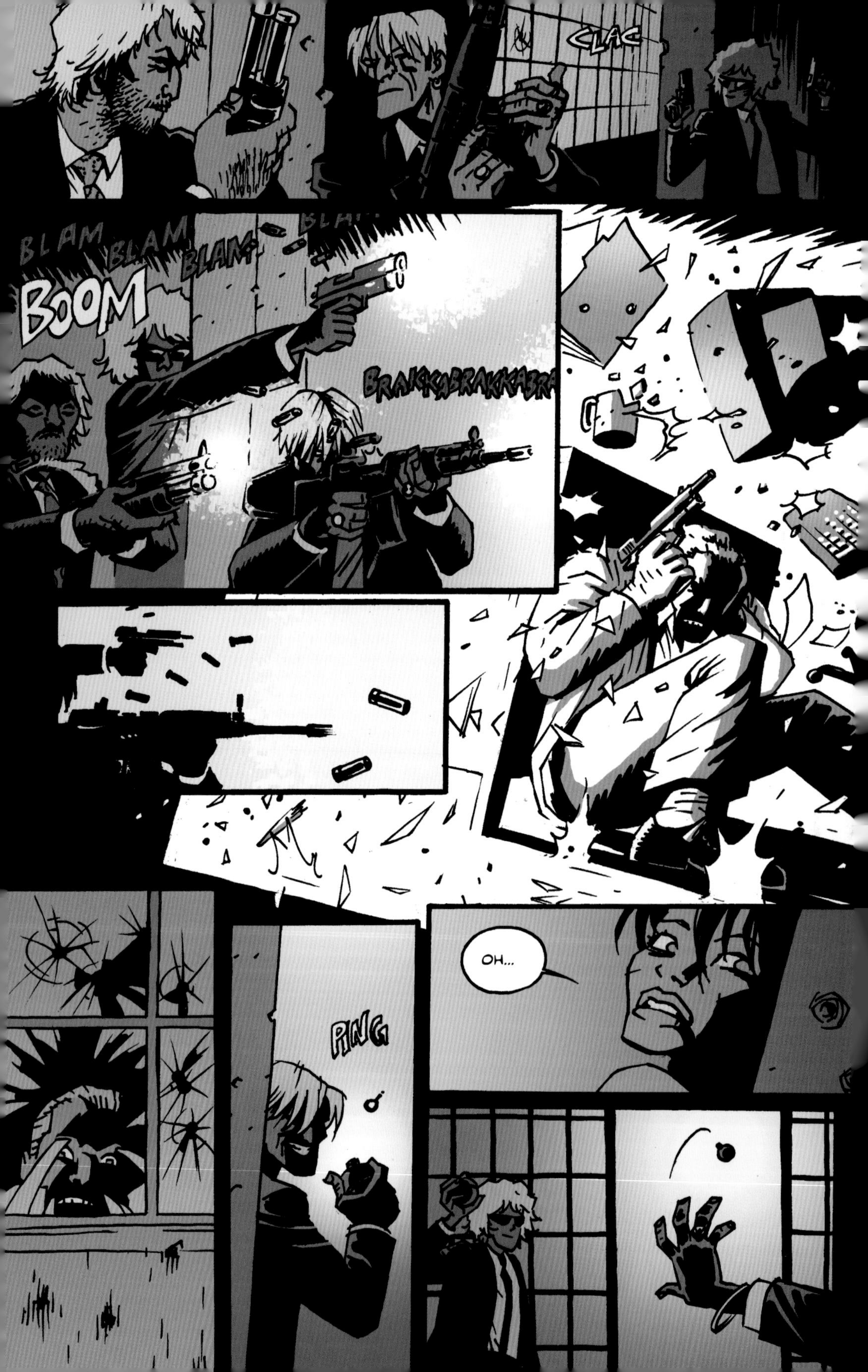
CLAC
BLAM
BLAM
BLAM
BLAM
BOOM
BRAKKABRAKKABRA
OH...
PING

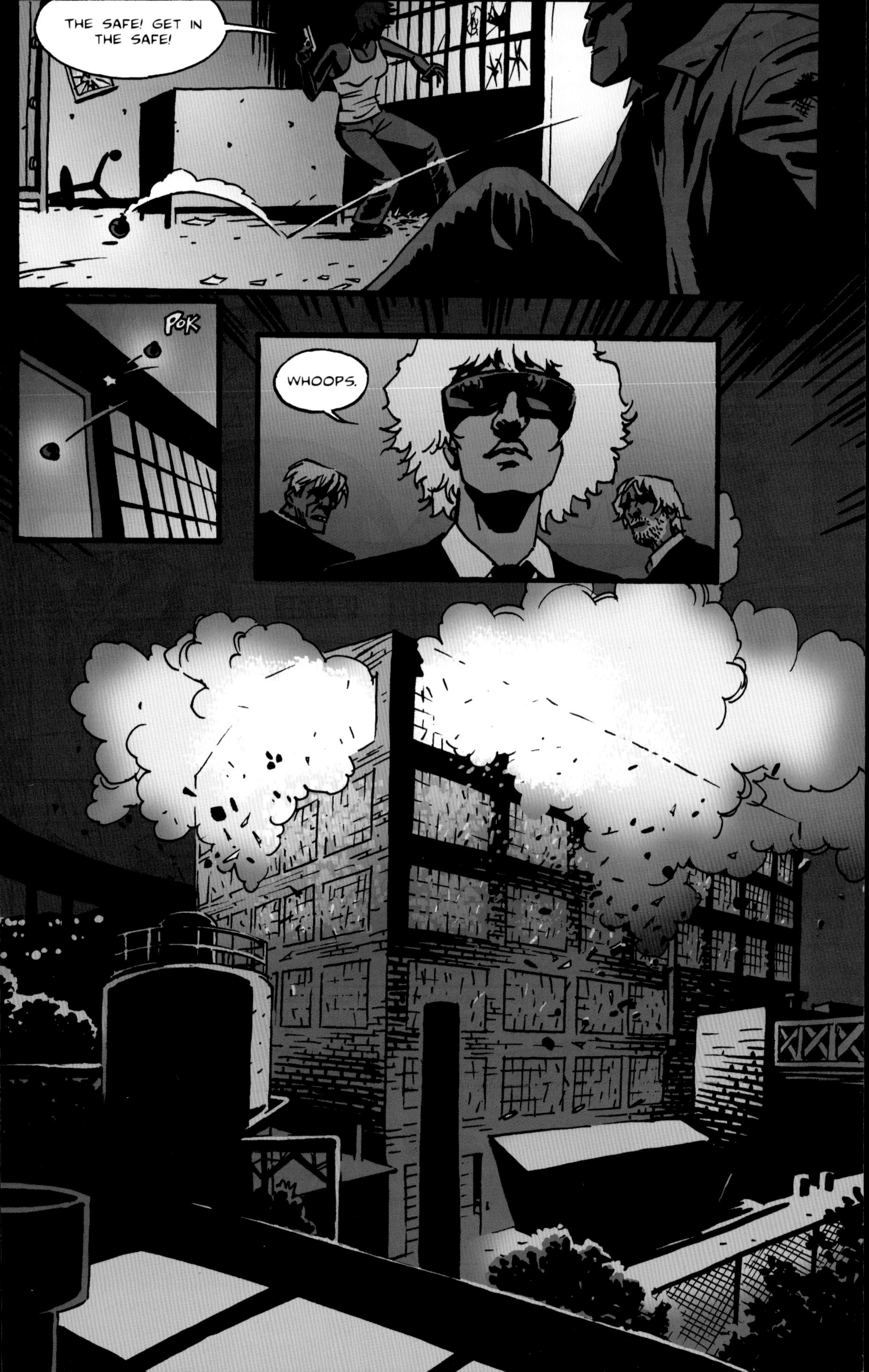
THE SAFE! GET IN THE SAFE!
POK
WHOOPS.

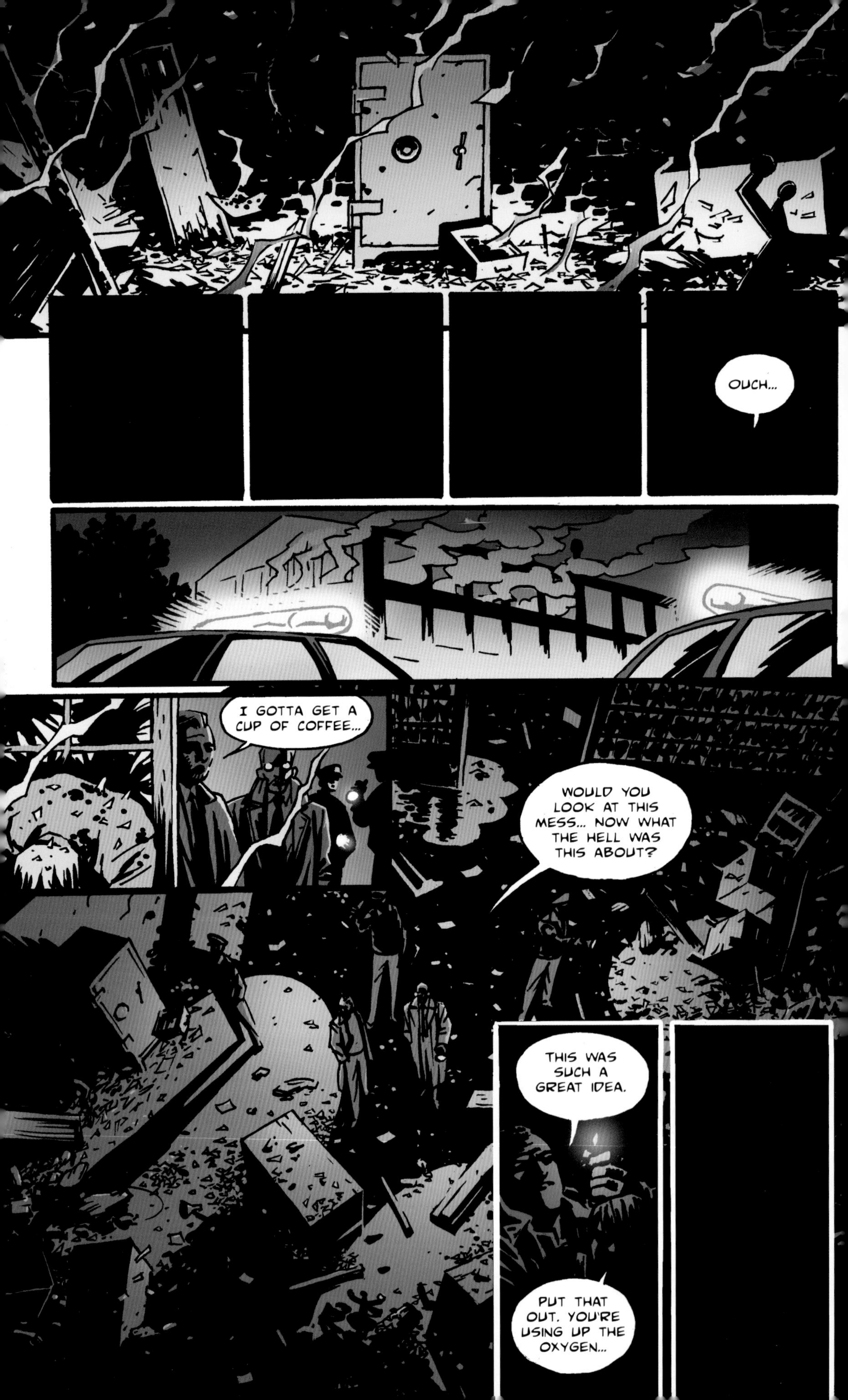
OUCH...
I GOTTA GET A CUP OF COFFEE...
WOULD YOU LOOK AT THIS MESS... NOW WHAT THE HELL WAS THIS ABOUT?
THIS WAS SUCH A GREAT IDEA.
PUT THAT OUT. YOU'RE USING UP THE OXYGEN...

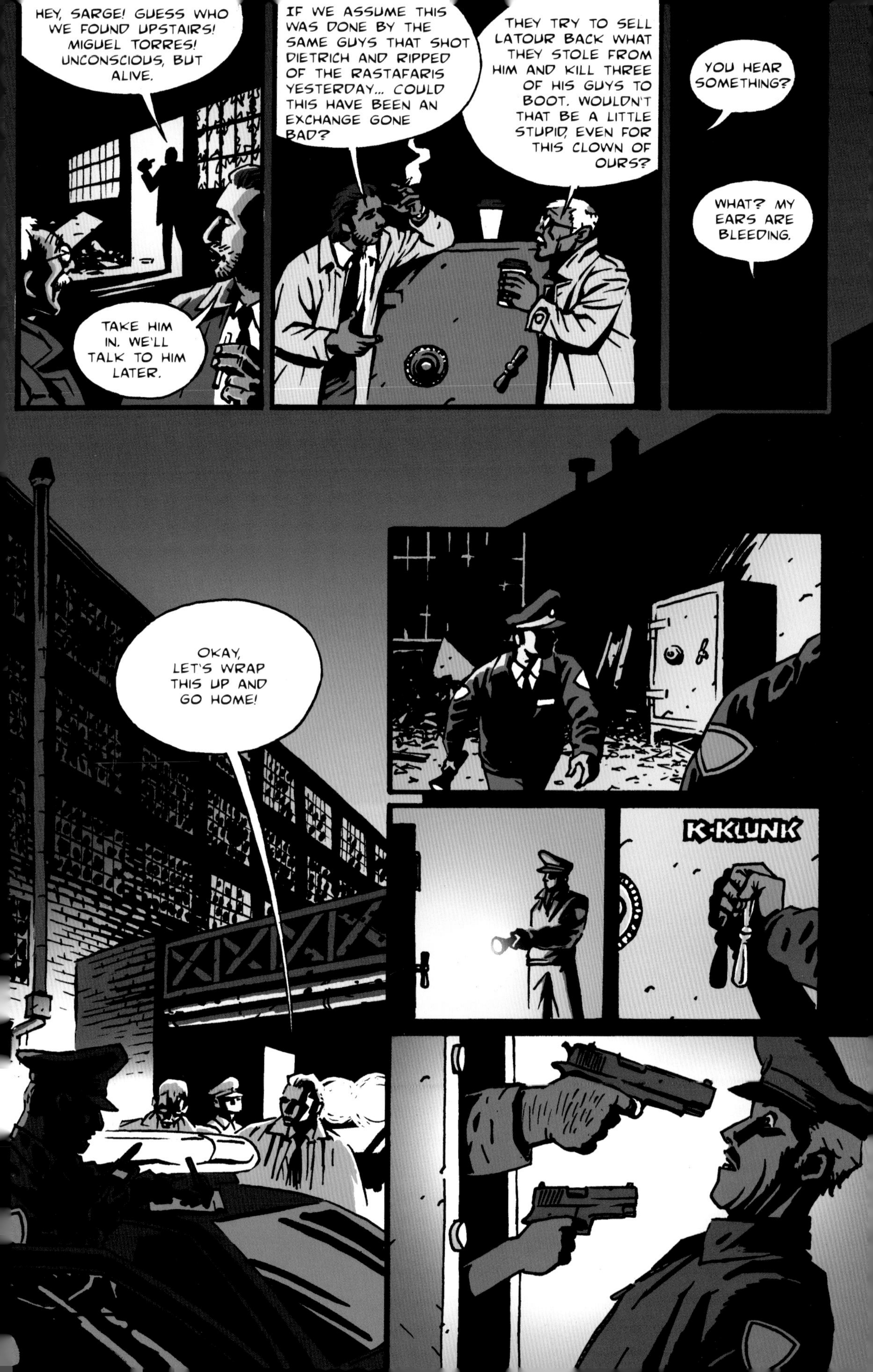
HEY, SARGE! GUESS WHO WE FOUND UPSTAIRS! MIGUEL TORRES! UNCONSCIOUS, BUT ALIVE.
TAKE HIM IN. WE'LL TALK TO HIM LATER.
IF WE ASSUME THIS WAS DONE BY THE SAME GUYS THAT SHOT DIETRICH AND RIPPED OF THE RASTAFARIS YESTERDAY... COULD THIS HAVE BEEN AN EXCHANGE GONE BAD?
THEY TRY TO SELL LATOUR BACK WHAT THEY STOLE FROM HIM AND KILL THREE OF HIS GUYS TO BOOT. WOULDN'T THAT BE A LITTLE STUPID, EVEN FOR THIS CLOWN OF OURS?
YOU HEAR SOMETHING?
WHAT? MY EARS ARE BLEEDING.
OKAY, LET'S WRAP THIS UP AND GO HOME!
K-KLUNK

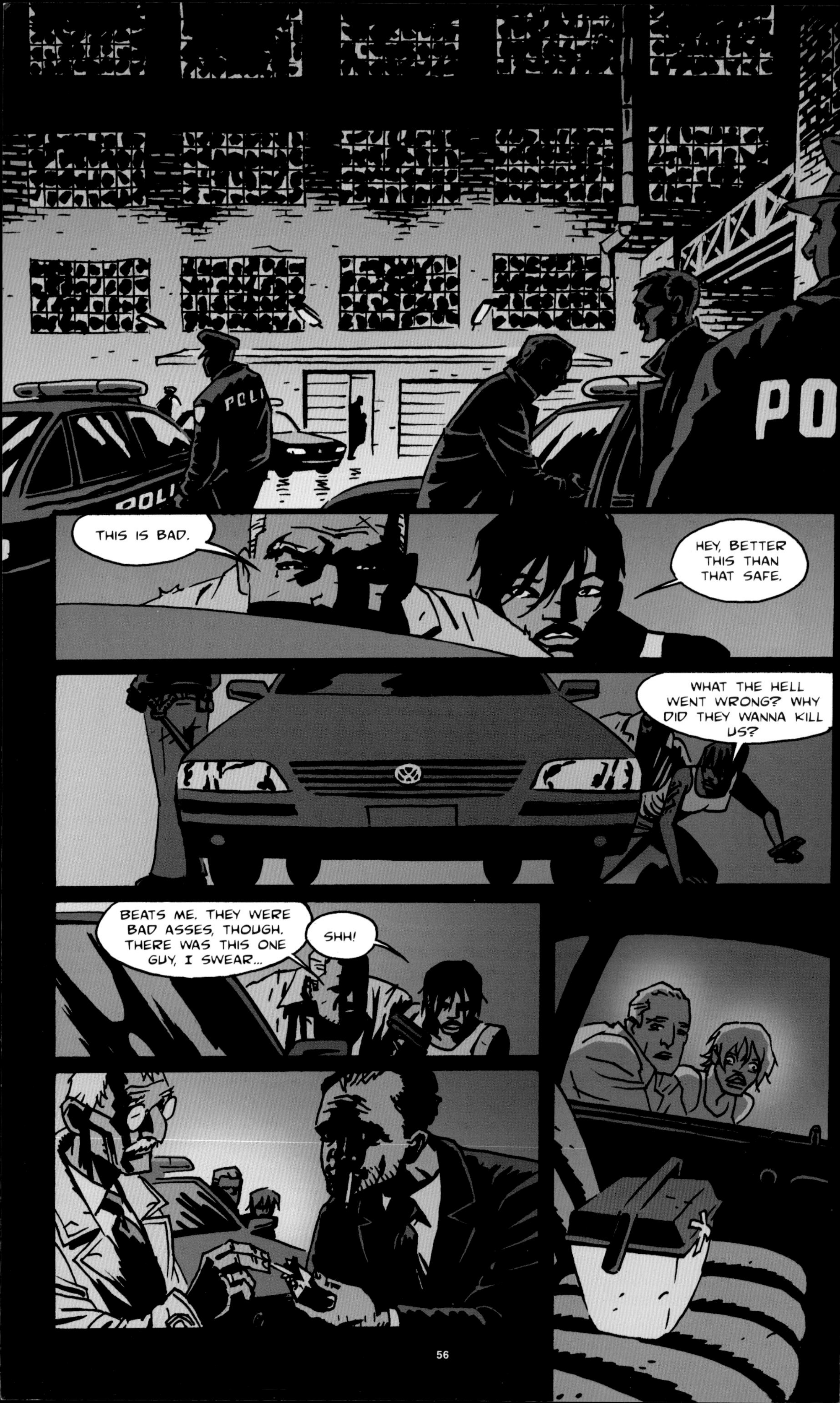
THIS IS BAD.
HEY, BETTER THIS THAN THAT SAFE.
WHAT THE HELL WENT WRONG? WHY DID THEY WANNA KILL US?
BEATS ME. THEY WERE BAD ASSES, THOUGH. THERE WAS THIS ONE GUY, I SWEAR...
SHH!

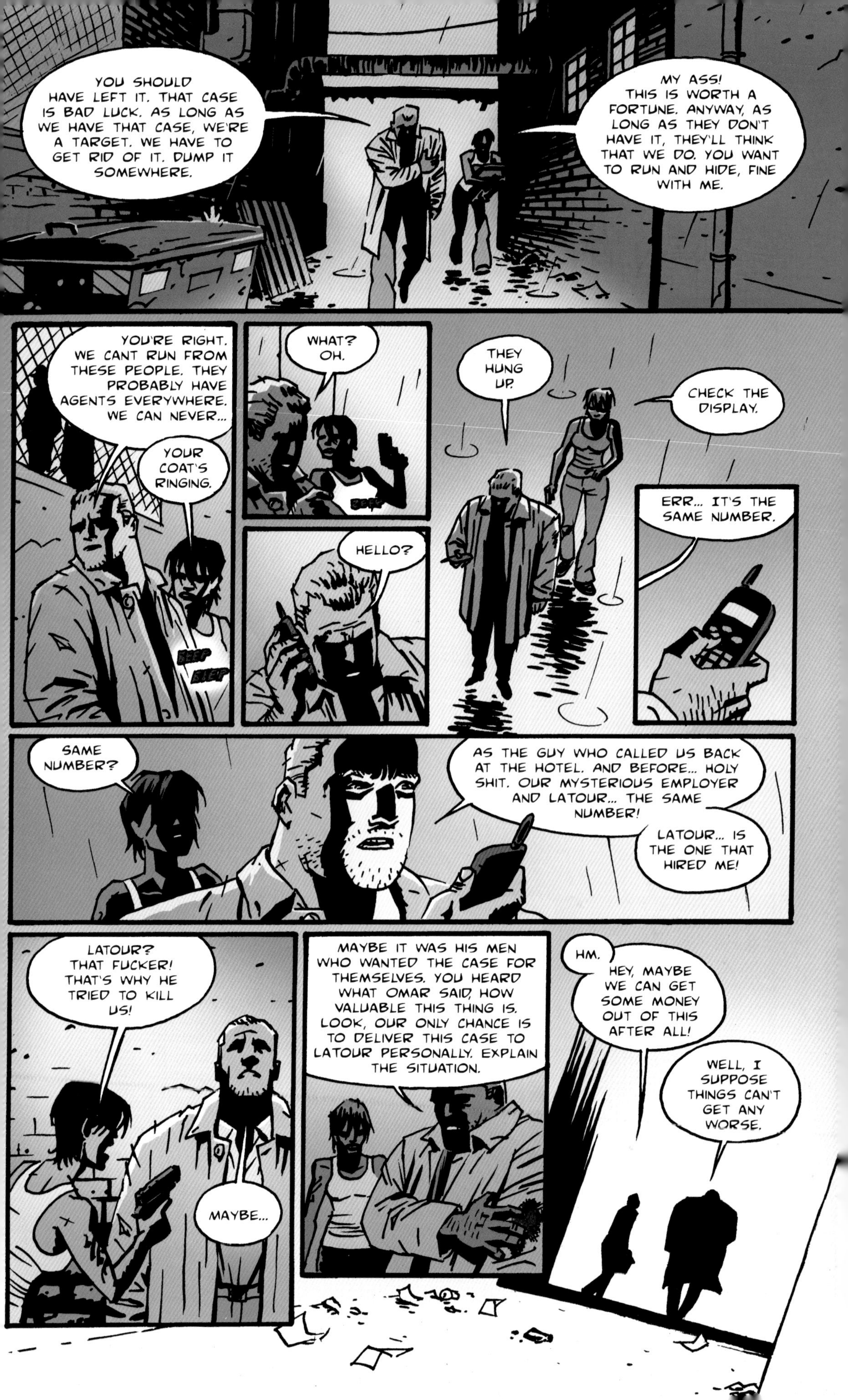
YOU SHOULD HAVE LEFT IT. THAT CASE IS BAD LUCK. AS LONG AS WE HAVE THAT CASE, WE'RE A TARGET. WE HAVE TO GET RID OF IT. DUMP IT SOMEWHERE.
MY ASS! THIS IS WORTH A FORTUNE. ANYWAY, AS LONG AS THEY DON'T HAVE IT, THEY'LL THINK THAT WE DO. YOU WANT TO RUN AND HIDE, FINE WITH ME.
YOU'RE RIGHT. WE CANT RUN FROM THESE PEOPLE. THEY PROBABLY HAVE AGENTS EVERYWHERE. WE CAN NEVER...
YOUR COAT'S RINGING.
WHAT? OH.
HELLO?
THEY HUNG UP.
CHECK THE DISPLAY.
ERR... IT'S THE SAME NUMBER.
SAME NUMBER?
AS THE GUY WHO CALLED US BACK AT THE HOTEL. AND BEFORE... HOLY SHIT. OUR MYSTERIOUS EMPLOYER AND LATOUR... THE SAME NUMBER!
LATOUR... IS THE ONE THAT HIRED ME!
LATOUR? THAT FUCKER! THAT'S WHY HE TRIED TO KILL US!
MAYBE...
MAYBE IT WAS HIS MEN WHO WANTED THE CASE FOR THEMSELVES. YOU HEARD WHAT OMAR SAID, HOW VALUABLE THIS THING IS. LOOK, OUR ONLY CHANCE IS TO DELIVER THIS CASE TO LATOUR PERSONALLY. EXPLAIN THE SITUATION.
HM.
HEY, MAYBE WE CAN GET SOME MONEY OUT OF THIS AFTER ALL!
WELL, I SUPPOSE THINGS CAN'T GET ANY WORSE.

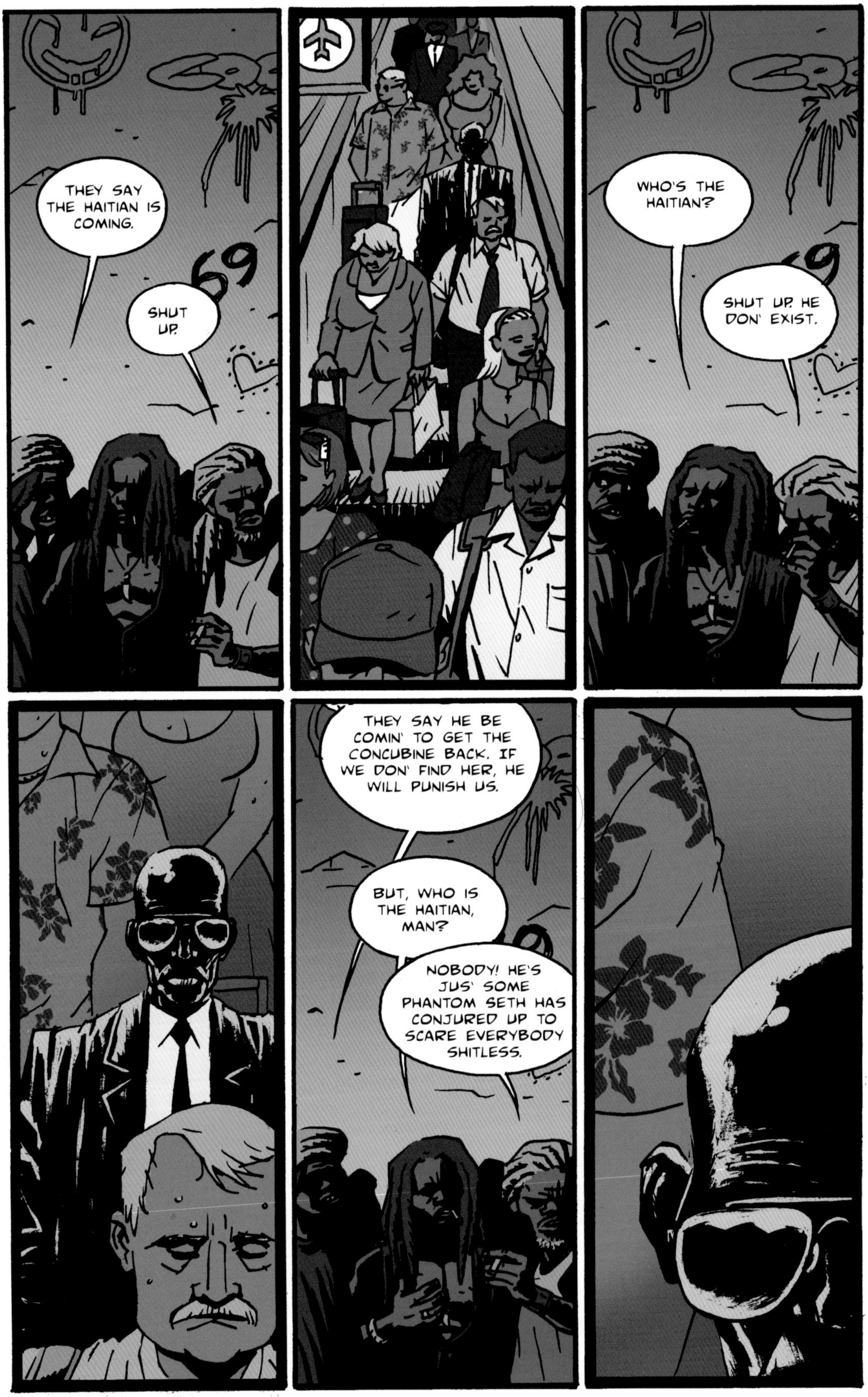
THEY SAY THE HAITIAN IS COMING.
SHUT UP.
WHO'S THE HAITIAN?
SHUT UP. HE DON' EXIST.
THEY SAY HE BE COMIN' TO GET THE CONCUBINE BACK. IF WE DON' FIND HER, HE WILL PUNISH US.
BUT, WHO IS THE HAITIAN, MAN?
NOBODY! HE'S JUS' SOME PHANTOM SETH HAS CONJURED UP TO SCARE EVERYBODY SHITLESS.

PART III

LIVE BY THE SWORD
DIE BY THE SWORD

"Mistakes were made.
I'm not denying that."
     –Jean-Luc

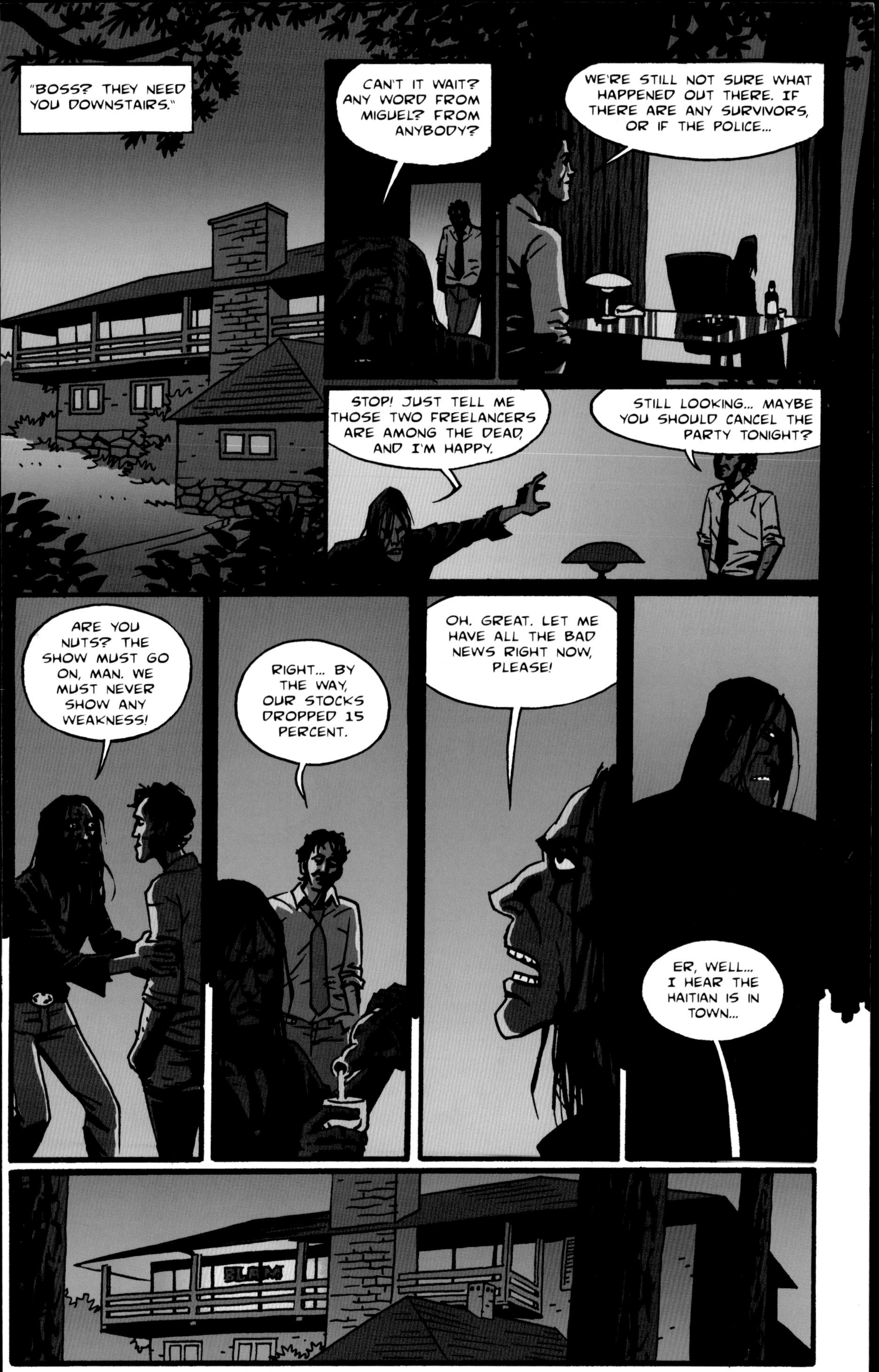
"BOSS? THEY NEED YOU DOWNSTAIRS."
CAN'T IT WAIT? ANY WORD FROM MIGUEL? FROM ANYBODY?
WE'RE STILL NOT SURE WHAT HAPPENED OUT THERE. IF THERE ARE ANY SURVIVORS, OR IF THE POLICE...
STOP! JUST TELL ME THOSE TWO FREELANCERS ARE AMONG THE DEAD, AND I'M HAPPY.
STILL LOOKING... MAYBE YOU SHOULD CANCEL THE PARTY TONIGHT?
ARE YOU NUTS? THE SHOW MUST GO ON, MAN. WE MUST NEVER SHOW ANY WEAKNESS!
RIGHT... BY THE WAY, OUR STOCKS DROPPED 15 PERCENT.
OH. GREAT. LET ME HAVE ALL THE BAD NEWS RIGHT NOW, PLEASE!
ER, WELL... I HEAR THE HAITIAN IS IN TOWN...
BLAM

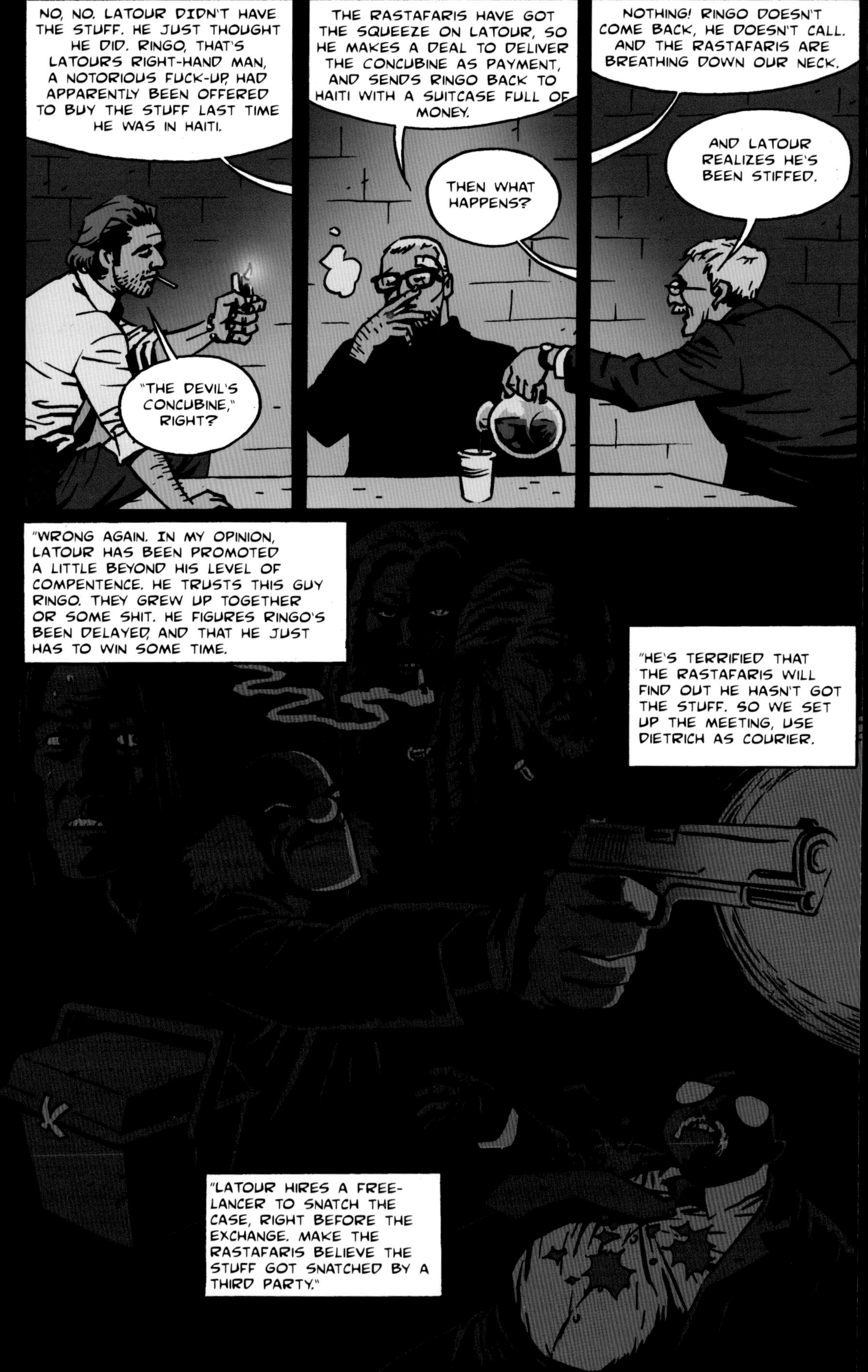
NO, NO. LATOUR DIDN'T HAVE THE STUFF. HE JUST THOUGHT HE DID. RINGO, THAT'S LATOURS RIGHT-HAND MAN, A NOTORIOUS FUCK-UP, HAD APPARENTLY BEEN OFFERED TO BUY THE STUFF LAST TIME HE WAS IN HAITI.
"THE DEVIL'S CONCUBINE," RIGHT?
THE RASTAFARIS HAVE GOT THE SQUEEZE ON LATOUR, SO HE MAKES A DEAL TO DELIVER THE CONCUBINE AS PAYMENT, AND SENDS RINGO BACK TO HAITI WITH A SUITCASE FULL OF MONEY.
THEN WHAT HAPPENS?
NOTHING! RINGO DOESN'T COME BACK, HE DOESN'T CALL. AND THE RASTAFARIS ARE BREATHING DOWN OUR NECK.
AND LATOUR REALIZES HE'S BEEN STIFFED.
"WRONG AGAIN. IN MY OPINION, LATOUR HAS BEEN PROMOTED A LITTLE BEYOND HIS LEVEL OF COMPENTENCE. HE TRUSTS THIS GUY RINGO. THEY GREW UP TOGETHER OR SOME SHIT. HE FIGURES RINGO'S BEEN DELAYED, AND THAT HE JUST HAS TO WIN SOME TIME.
"HE'S TERRIFIED THAT THE RASTAFARIS WILL FIND OUT HE HASN'T GOT THE STUFF. SO WE SET UP THE MEETING, USE DIETRICH AS COURIER.
"LATOUR HIRES A FREE-LANCER TO SNATCH THE CASE, RIGHT BEFORE THE EXCHANGE. MAKE THE RASTAFARIS BELIEVE THE STUFF GOT SNATCHED BY A THIRD PARTY."

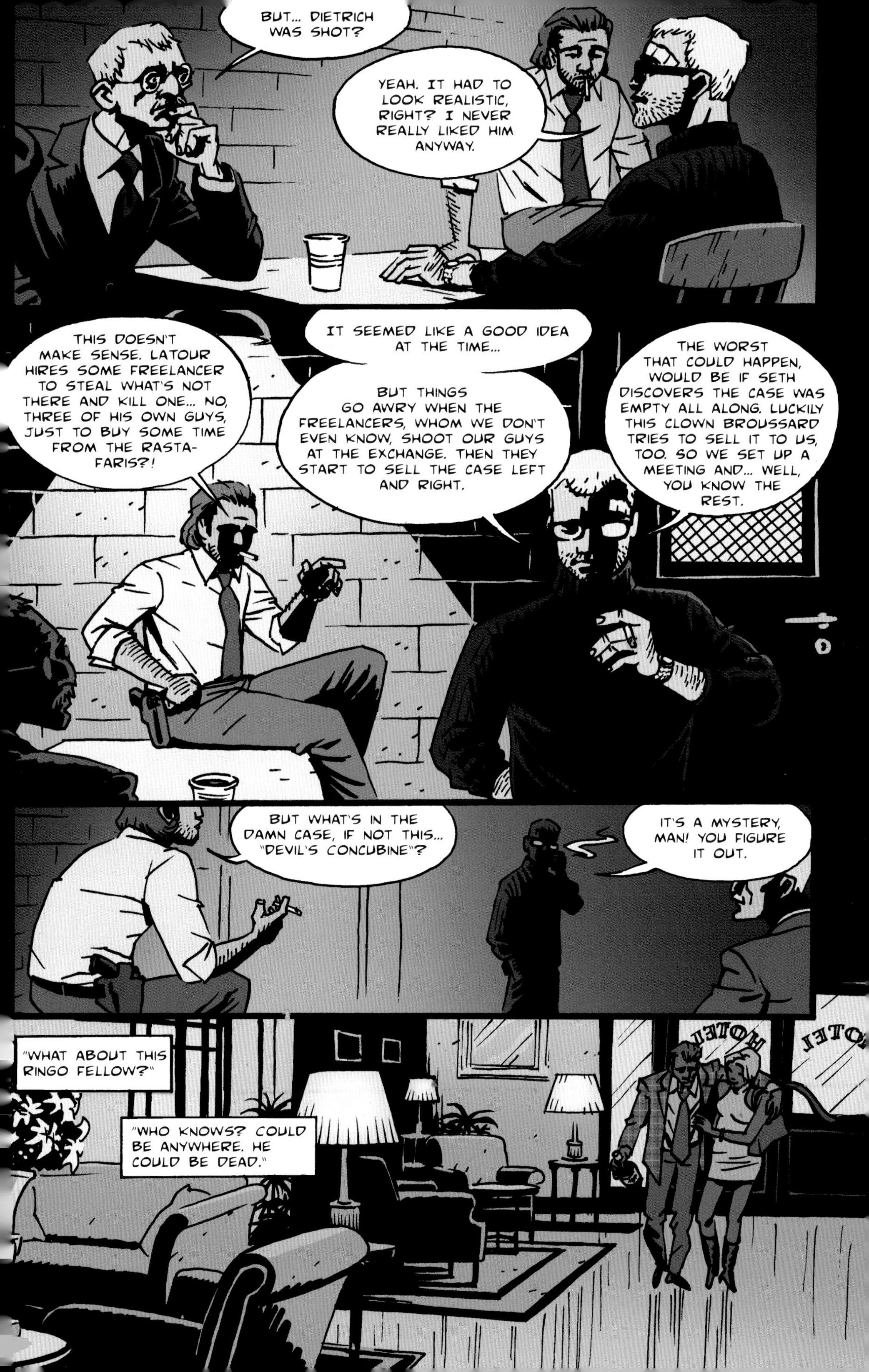

BUT... DIETRICH WAS SHOT?
YEAH. IT HAD TO LOOK REALISTIC, RIGHT? I NEVER REALLY LIKED HIM ANYWAY.
THIS DOESN'T MAKE SENSE. LATOUR HIRES SOME FREELANCER TO STEAL WHAT'S NOT THERE AND KILL ONE... NO, THREE OF HIS OWN GUYS, JUST TO BUY SOME TIME FROM THE RASTA-FARIS?!
IT SEEMED LIKE A GOOD IDEA AT THE TIME...
BUT THINGS GO AWRY WHEN THE FREELANCERS, WHOM WE DON'T EVEN KNOW, SHOOT OUR GUYS AT THE EXCHANGE. THEN THEY START TO SELL THE CASE LEFT AND RIGHT.
THE WORST THAT COULD HAPPEN, WOULD BE IF SETH DISCOVERS THE CASE WAS EMPTY ALL ALONG. LUCKILY THIS CLOWN BROUSSARD TRIES TO SELL IT TO US, TOO. SO WE SET UP A MEETING AND... WELL, YOU KNOW THE REST.
BUT WHAT'S IN THE DAMN CASE, IF NOT THIS... "DEVIL'S CONCUBINE"?
IT'S A MYSTERY, MAN! YOU FIGURE IT OUT.
"WHAT ABOUT THIS RINGO FELLOW?"
"WHO KNOWS? COULD BE ANYWHERE. HE COULD BE DEAD."

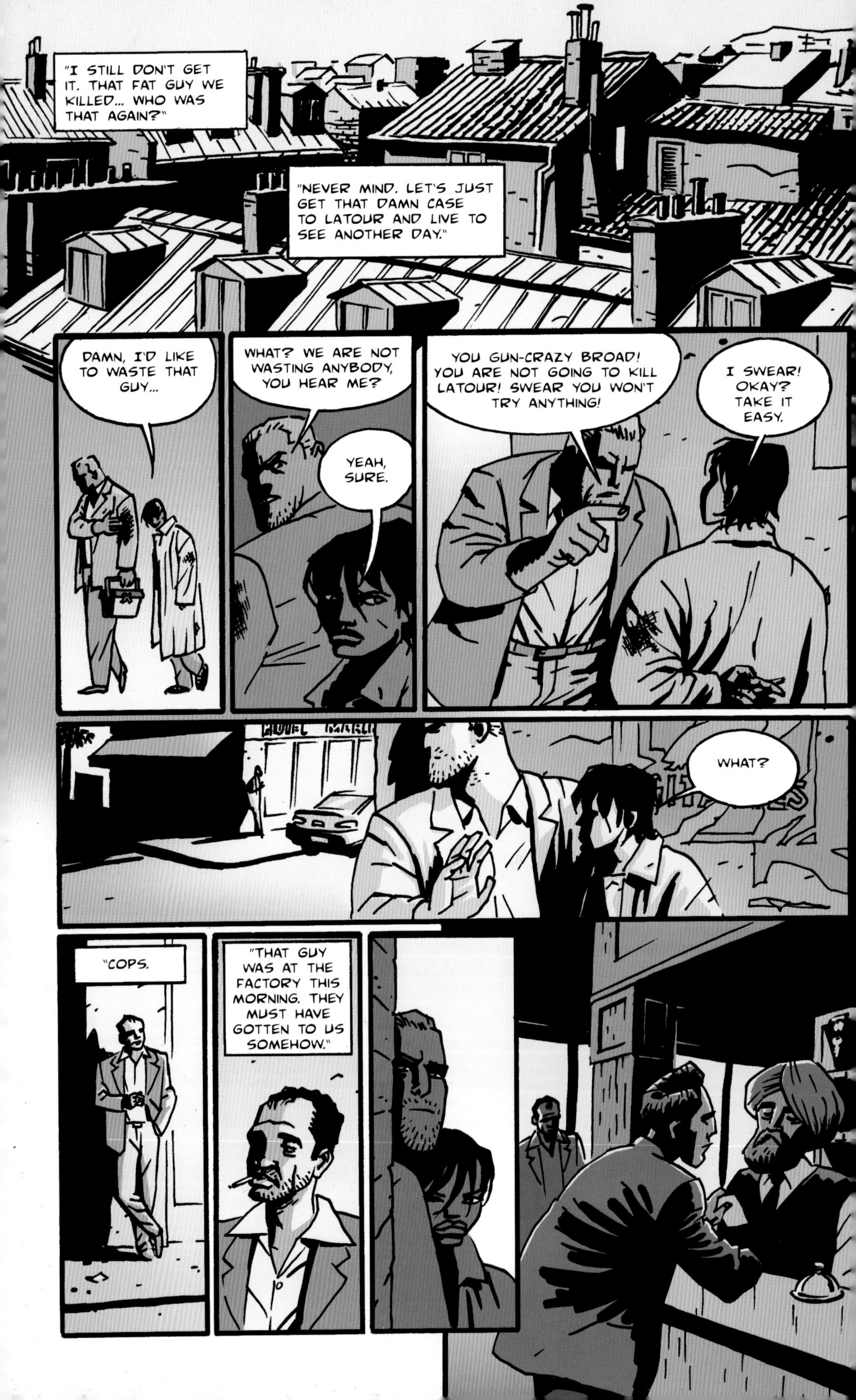
"I STILL DON'T GET IT. THAT FAT GUY WE KILLED... WHO WAS THAT AGAIN?"
"NEVER MIND. LET'S JUST GET THAT DAMN CASE TO LATOUR AND LIVE TO SEE ANOTHER DAY."
DAMN, I'D LIKE TO WASTE THAT GUY...
WHAT? WE ARE NOT WASTING ANYBODY, YOU HEAR ME?
YEAH, SURE.
YOU GUN-CRAZY BROAD! YOU ARE NOT GOING TO KILL LATOUR! SWEAR YOU WON'T TRY ANYTHING!
I SWEAR! OKAY? TAKE IT EASY.
WHAT?
"COPS.
"THAT GUY WAS AT THE FACTORY THIS MORNING. THEY MUST HAVE GOTTEN TO US SOMEHOW."

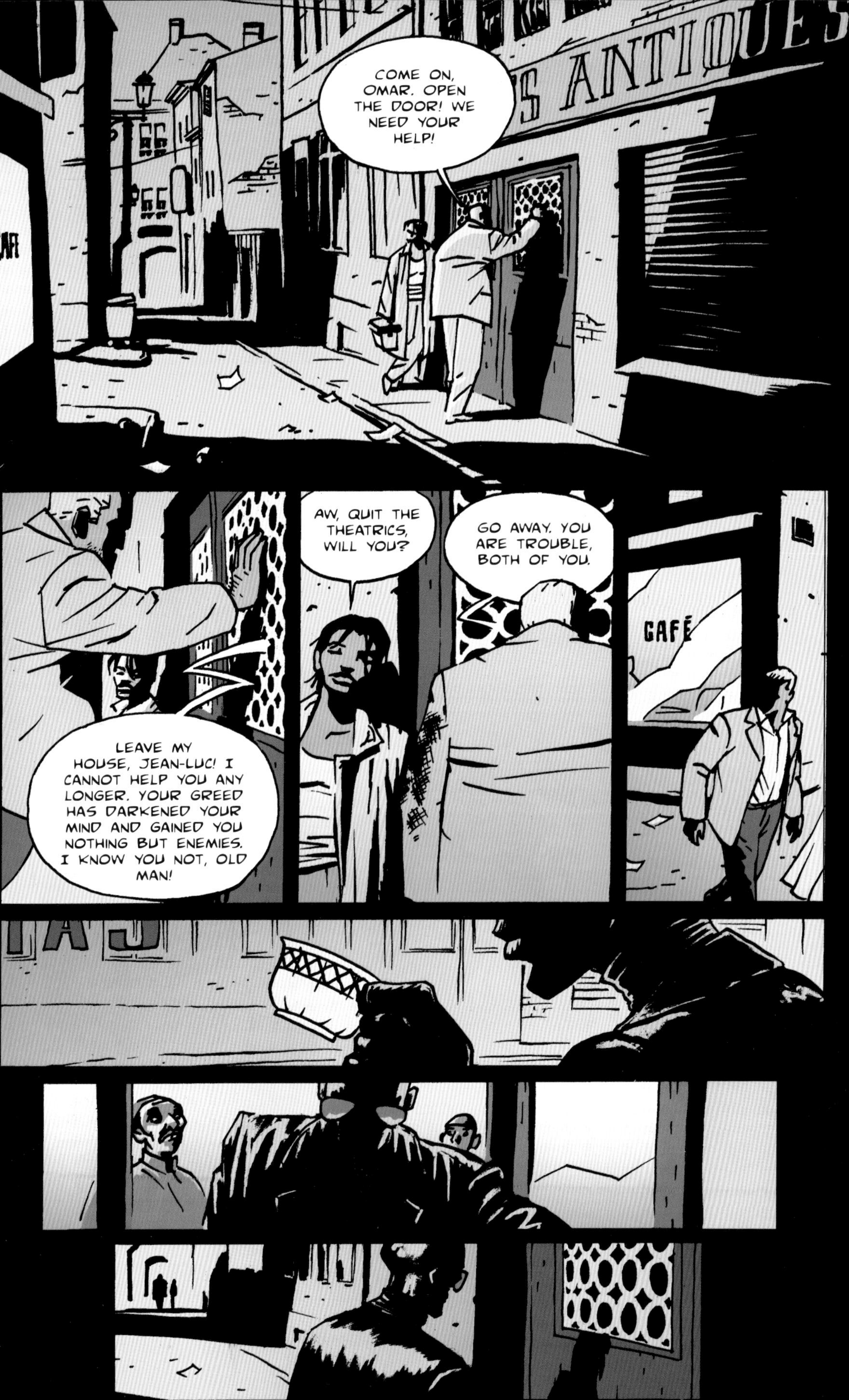

ANTIQUES
CAFE
COME ON, OMAR. OPEN THE DOOR! WE NEED YOUR HELP!
AW, QUIT THE THEATRICS, WILL YOU?
GO AWAY. YOU ARE TROUBLE, BOTH OF YOU.
CAFÉ
LEAVE MY HOUSE, JEAN-LUC! I CANNOT HELP YOU ANY LONGER. YOUR GREED HAS DARKENED YOUR MIND AND GAINED YOU NOTHING BUT ENEMIES. I KNOW YOU NOT, OLD MAN!

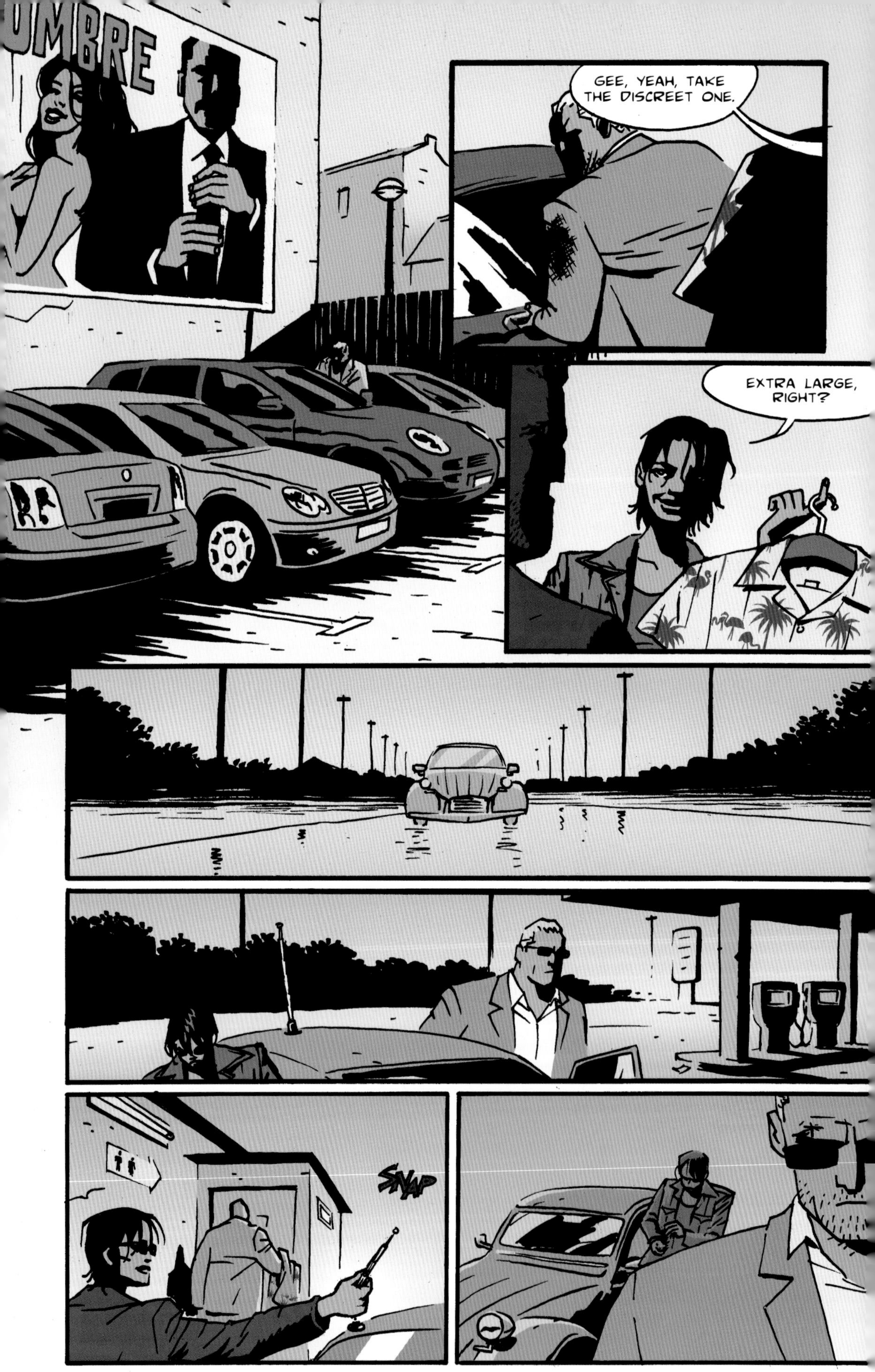
UMBRE
GEE, YEAH, TAKE THE DISCREET ONE.
EXTRA LARGE, RIGHT?
SNAP

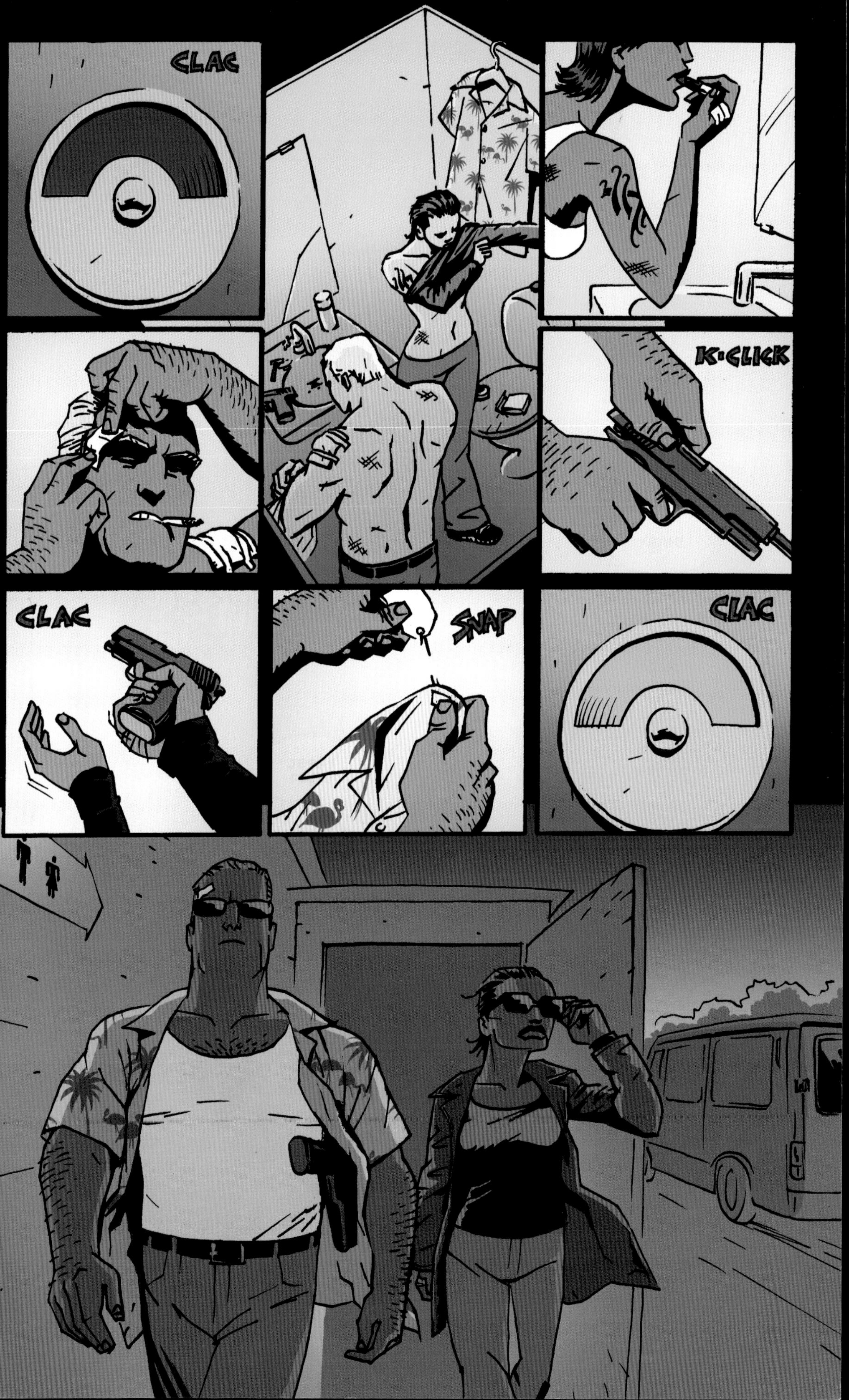
CLAC
K-CLICK
CLAC
SNAP
CLAC

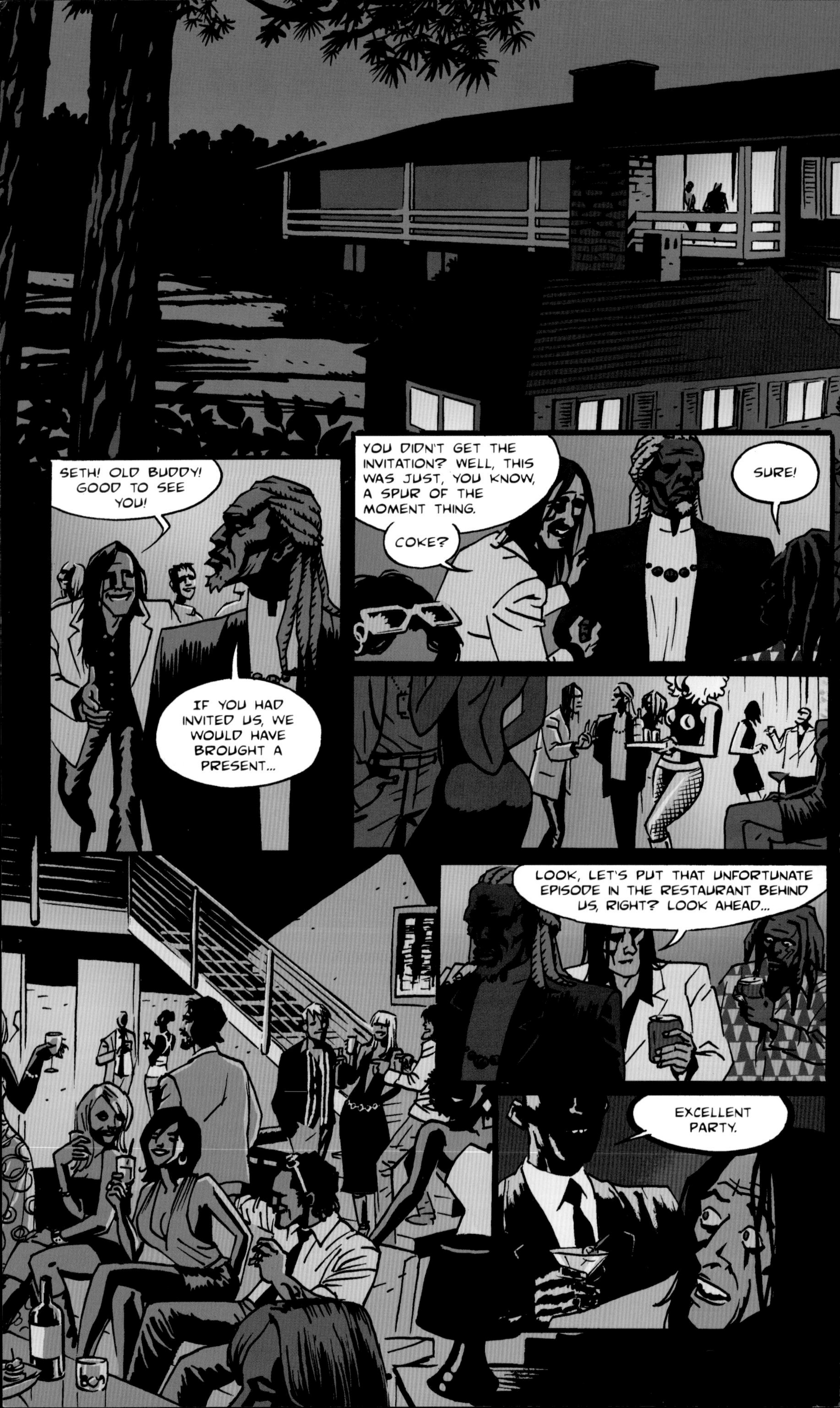
SETH! OLD BUDDY! GOOD TO SEE YOU!
IF YOU HAD INVITED US, WE WOULD HAVE BROUGHT A PRESENT...
YOU DIDN'T GET THE INVITATION? WELL, THIS WAS JUST, YOU KNOW, A SPUR OF THE MOMENT THING.
COKE?
SURE!
LOOK, LET'S PUT THAT UNFORTUNATE EPISODE IN THE RESTAURANT BEHIND US, RIGHT? LOOK AHEAD...
EXCELLENT PARTY.

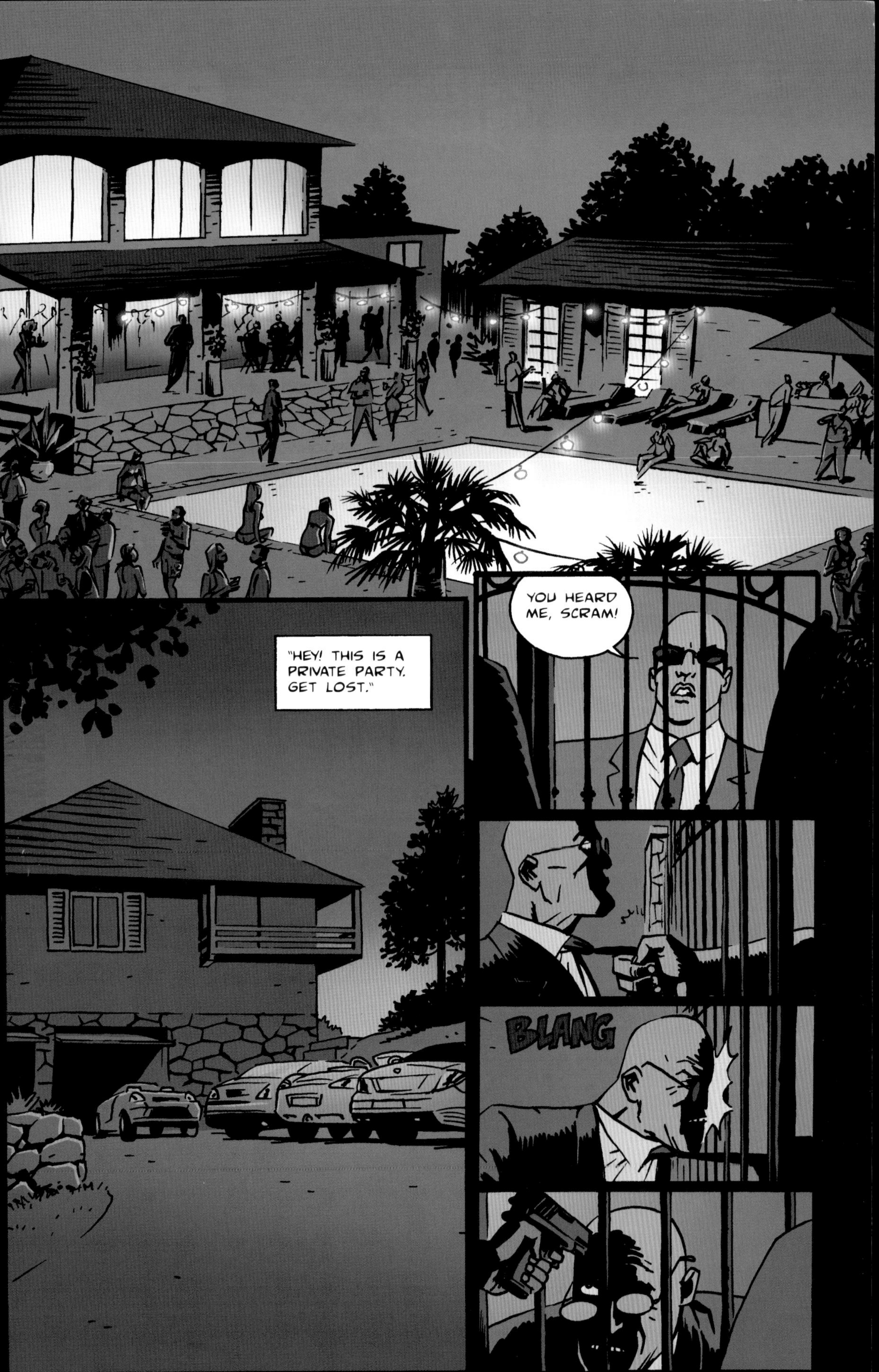
"HEY! THIS IS A PRIVATE PARTY. GET LOST."
YOU HEARD ME, SCRAM!
BLANG

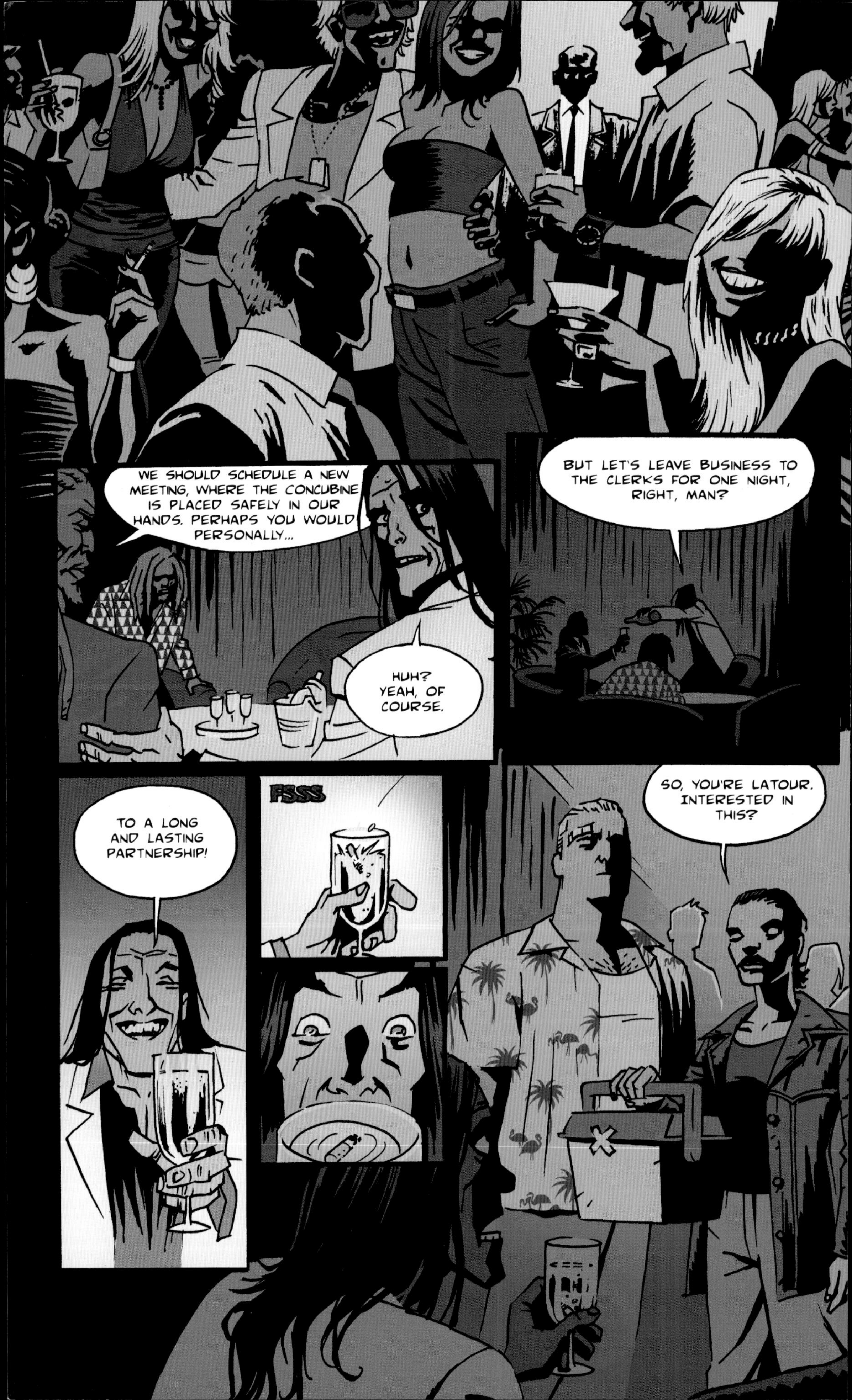
WE SHOULD SCHEDULE A NEW MEETING, WHERE THE CONCUBINE IS PLACED SAFELY IN OUR HANDS. PERHAPS YOU WOULD PERSONALLY...
HUH? YEAH, OF COURSE.
BUT LET'S LEAVE BUSINESS TO THE CLERKS FOR ONE NIGHT, RIGHT, MAN?
TO A LONG AND LASTING PARTNERSHIP!
FSSS
SO, YOU'RE LATOUR. INTERESTED IN THIS?

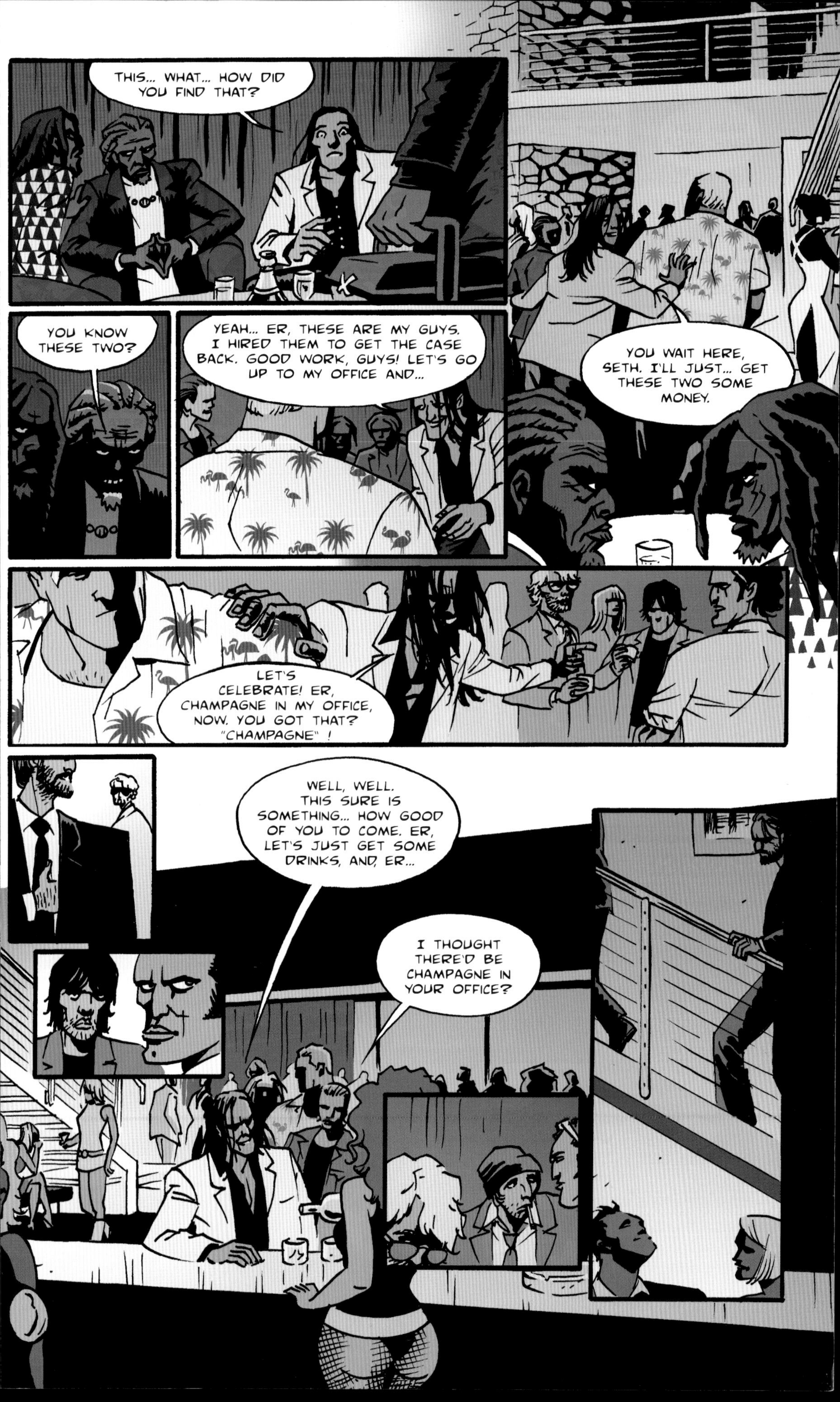
THIS... WHAT... HOW DID YOU FIND THAT?
YOU KNOW THESE TWO?
YEAH... ER, THESE ARE MY GUYS. I HIRED THEM TO GET THE CASE BACK. GOOD WORK, GUYS! LET'S GO UP TO MY OFFICE AND...
YOU WAIT HERE, SETH. I'LL JUST... GET THESE TWO SOME MONEY.
LET'S CELEBRATE! ER, CHAMPAGNE IN MY OFFICE, NOW. YOU GOT THAT? "CHAMPAGNE"!
WELL, WELL. THIS SURE IS SOMETHING... HOW GOOD OF YOU TO COME. ER, LET'S JUST GET SOME DRINKS, AND, ER...
I THOUGHT THERE'D BE CHAMPAGNE IN YOUR OFFICE?

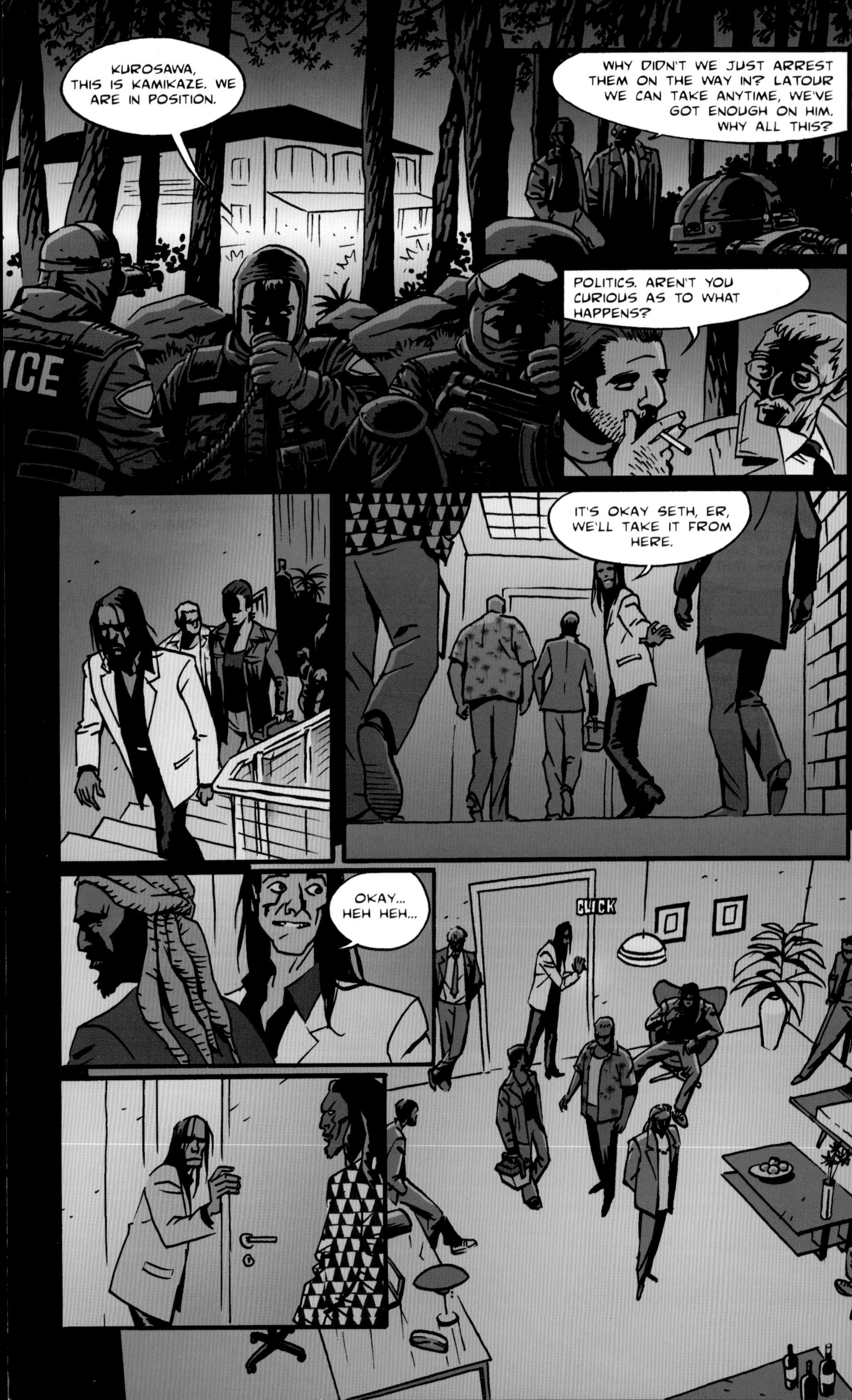
KUROSAWA, THIS IS KAMIKAZE. WE ARE IN POSITION.
WHY DIDN'T WE JUST ARREST THEM ON THE WAY IN? LATOUR WE CAN TAKE ANYTIME, WE'VE GOT ENOUGH ON HIM. WHY ALL THIS?
POLITICS. AREN'T YOU CURIOUS AS TO WHAT HAPPENS?
IT'S OKAY SETH, ER, WE'LL TAKE IT FROM HERE.
OKAY... HEH HEH...
CLICK

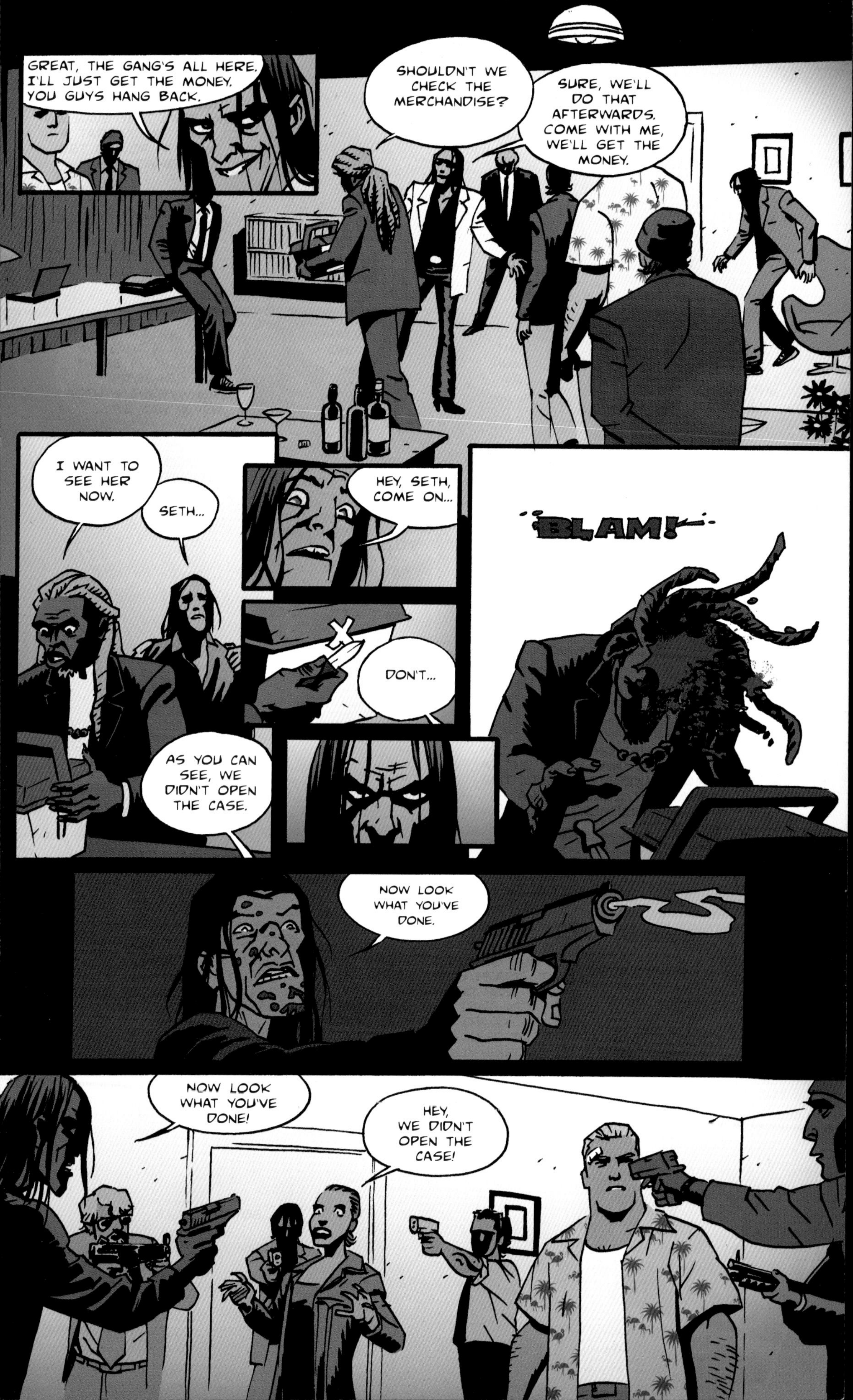
GREAT, THE GANG'S ALL HERE. I'LL JUST GET THE MONEY. YOU GUYS HANG BACK.
SHOULDN'T WE CHECK THE MERCHANDISE?
SURE, WE'LL DO THAT AFTERWARDS. COME WITH ME, WE'LL GET THE MONEY.
I WANT TO SEE HER NOW.
SETH...
HEY, SETH, COME ON...
DON'T...
AS YOU CAN SEE, WE DIDN'T OPEN THE CASE.
BLAM!
NOW LOOK WHAT YOU'VE DONE.
NOW LOOK WHAT YOU'VE DONE!
HEY, WE DIDN'T OPEN THE CASE!

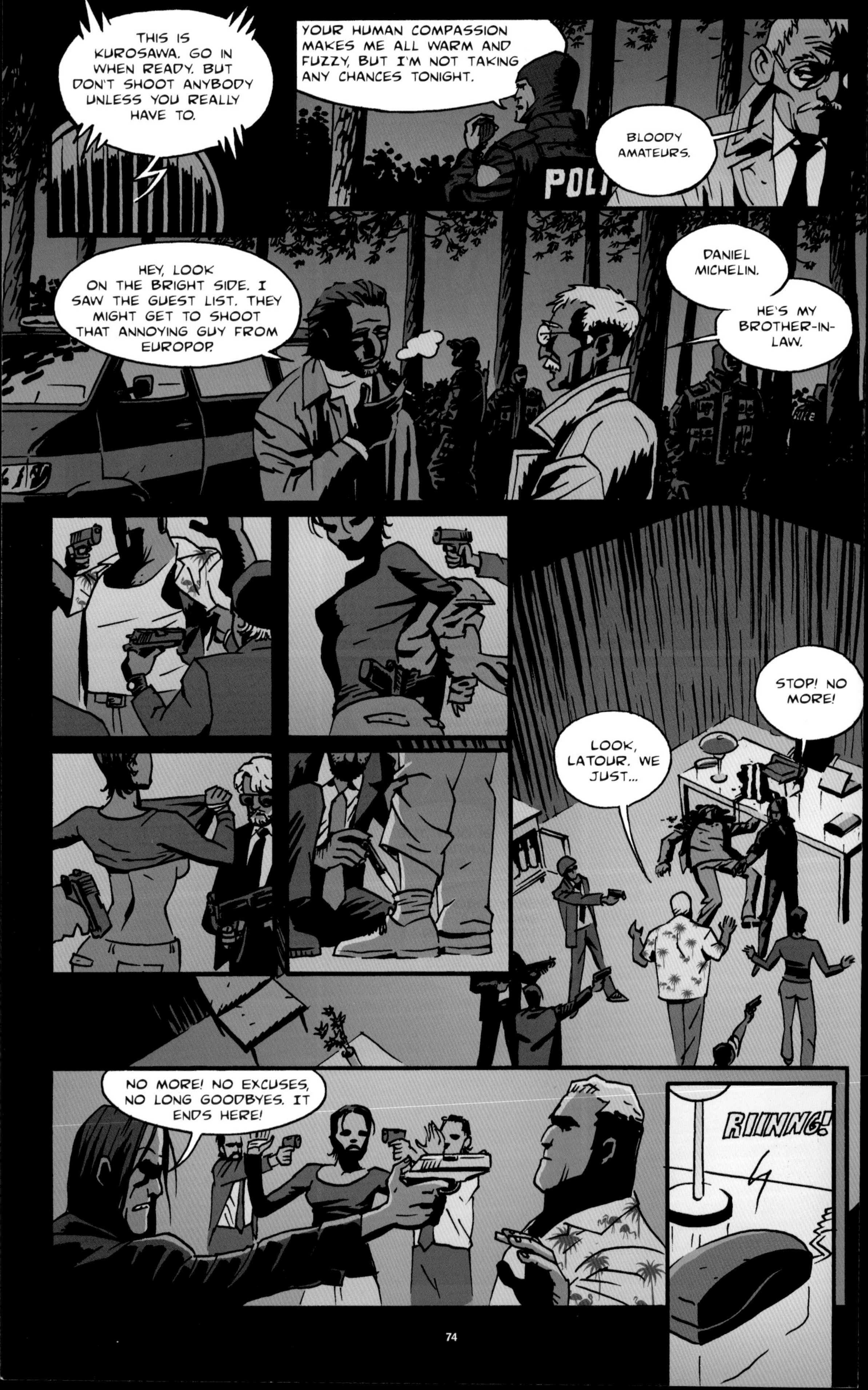
THIS IS KUROSAWA. GO IN WHEN READY. BUT DON'T SHOOT ANYBODY UNLESS YOU REALLY HAVE TO.
YOUR HUMAN COMPASSION MAKES ME ALL WARM AND FUZZY, BUT I'M NOT TAKING ANY CHANCES TONIGHT.
POLI
BLOODY AMATEURS.
HEY, LOOK ON THE BRIGHT SIDE. I SAW THE GUEST LIST. THEY MIGHT GET TO SHOOT THAT ANNOYING GUY FROM EUROPOP.
DANIEL MICHELIN.
HE'S MY BROTHER-IN-LAW.
LOOK, LATOUR. WE JUST...
STOP! NO MORE!
NO MORE! NO EXCUSES, NO LONG GOODBYES. IT ENDS HERE!
RIIINNG!

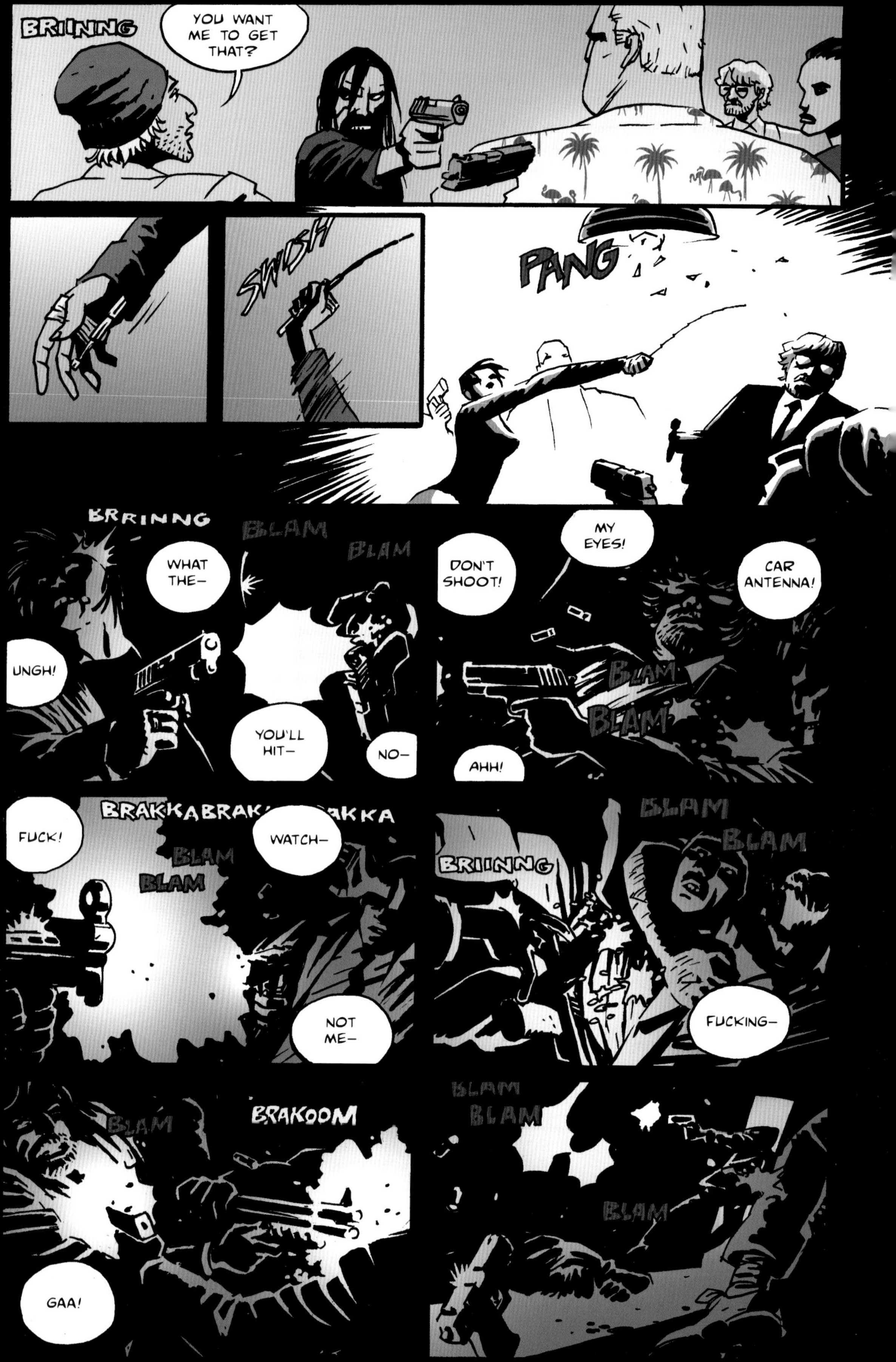
BRIINNG
YOU WANT ME TO GET THAT?
SWISH
PANG
BRRINNG
WHAT THE–
UNGH!
BLAM
BLAM
YOU'LL HIT–
NO–
MY EYES!
DON'T SHOOT!
CAR ANTENNA!
BLAM
BLAM
AHH!
BRAKKABRAK BRAKKA
FUCK!
WATCH–
BLAM
BLAM
NOT ME–
BLAM
BLAM
BRIINNG
FUCKING–
BLAM
BRAKOOM
GAA!
BLAM
BLAM
BLAM

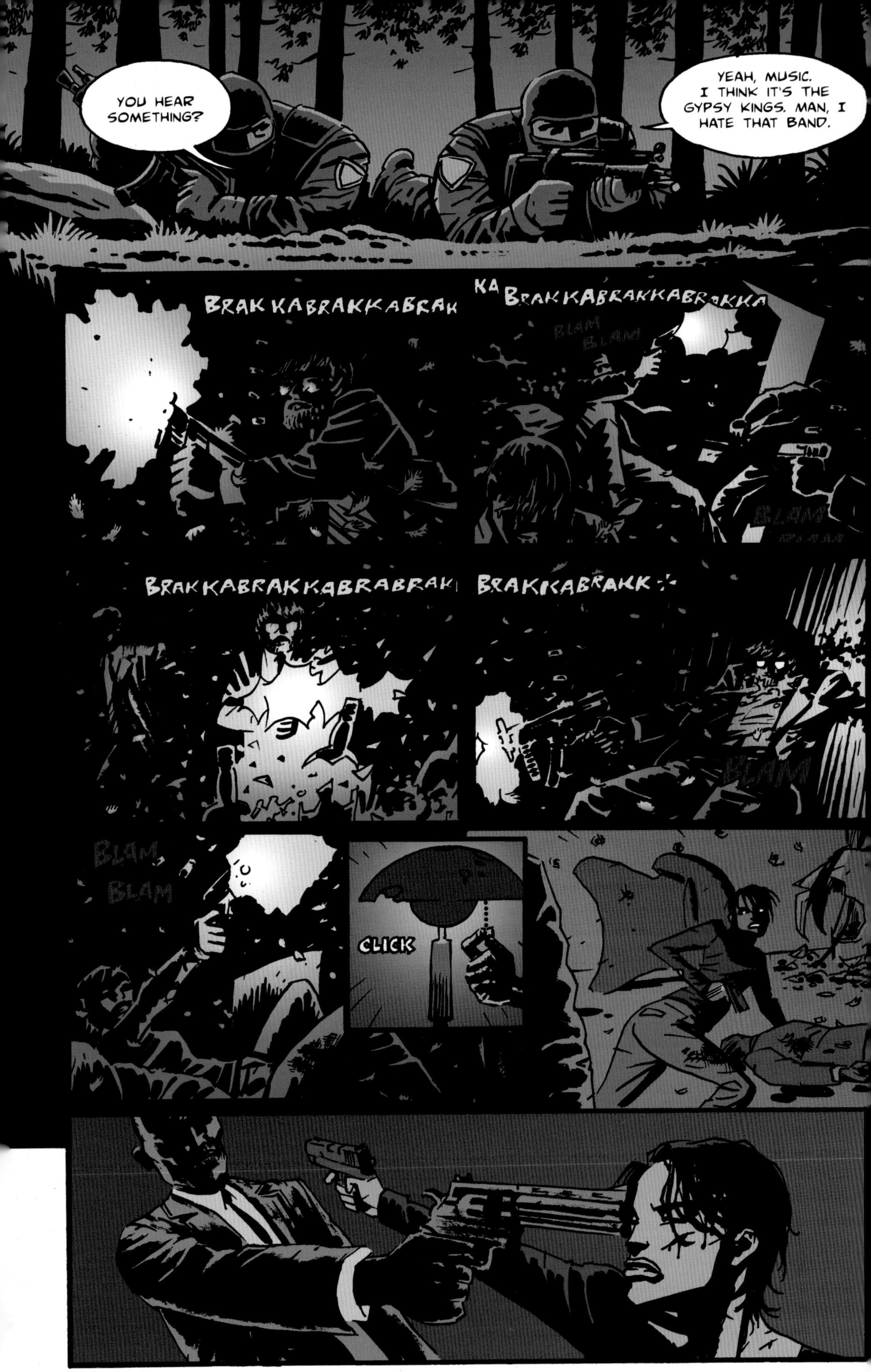
YOU HEAR SOMETHING?
YEAH, MUSIC. I THINK IT'S THE GYPSY KINGS. MAN, I HATE THAT BAND.
BRAKKABRAKKABRAK
KA BRAKKABRAKKABRAKKA
BLAM BLAM
BLAM
BRAKKABRAKKABRABRAK
BRAKKABRAKK
BLAM
BLAM, BLAM
CLICK

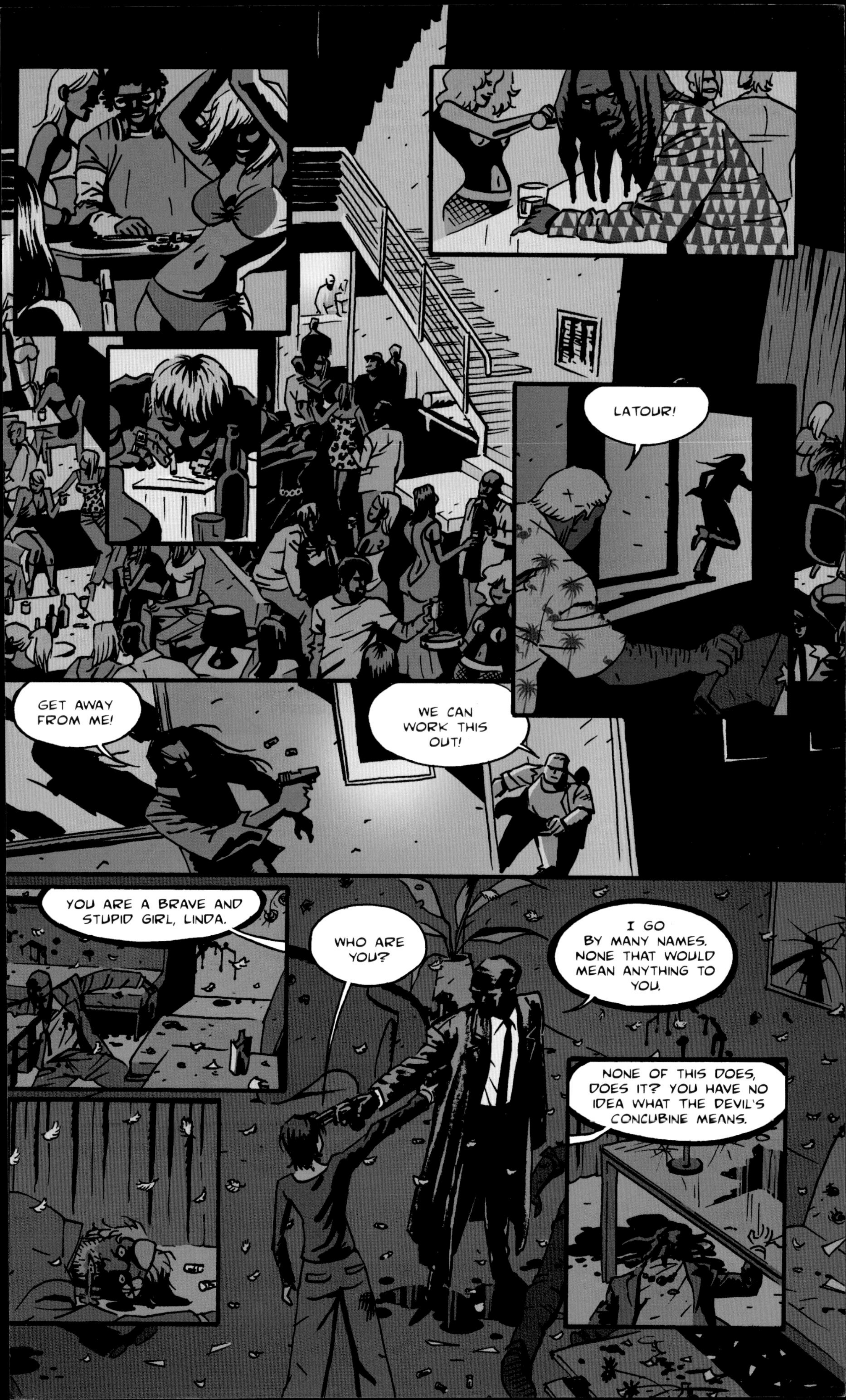
LATOUR!
GET AWAY FROM ME!
WE CAN WORK THIS OUT!
YOU ARE A BRAVE AND STUPID GIRL, LINDA.
WHO ARE YOU?
I GO BY MANY NAMES. NONE THAT WOULD MEAN ANYTHING TO YOU.
NONE OF THIS DOES, DOES IT? YOU HAVE NO IDEA WHAT THE DEVIL'S CONCUBINE MEANS.

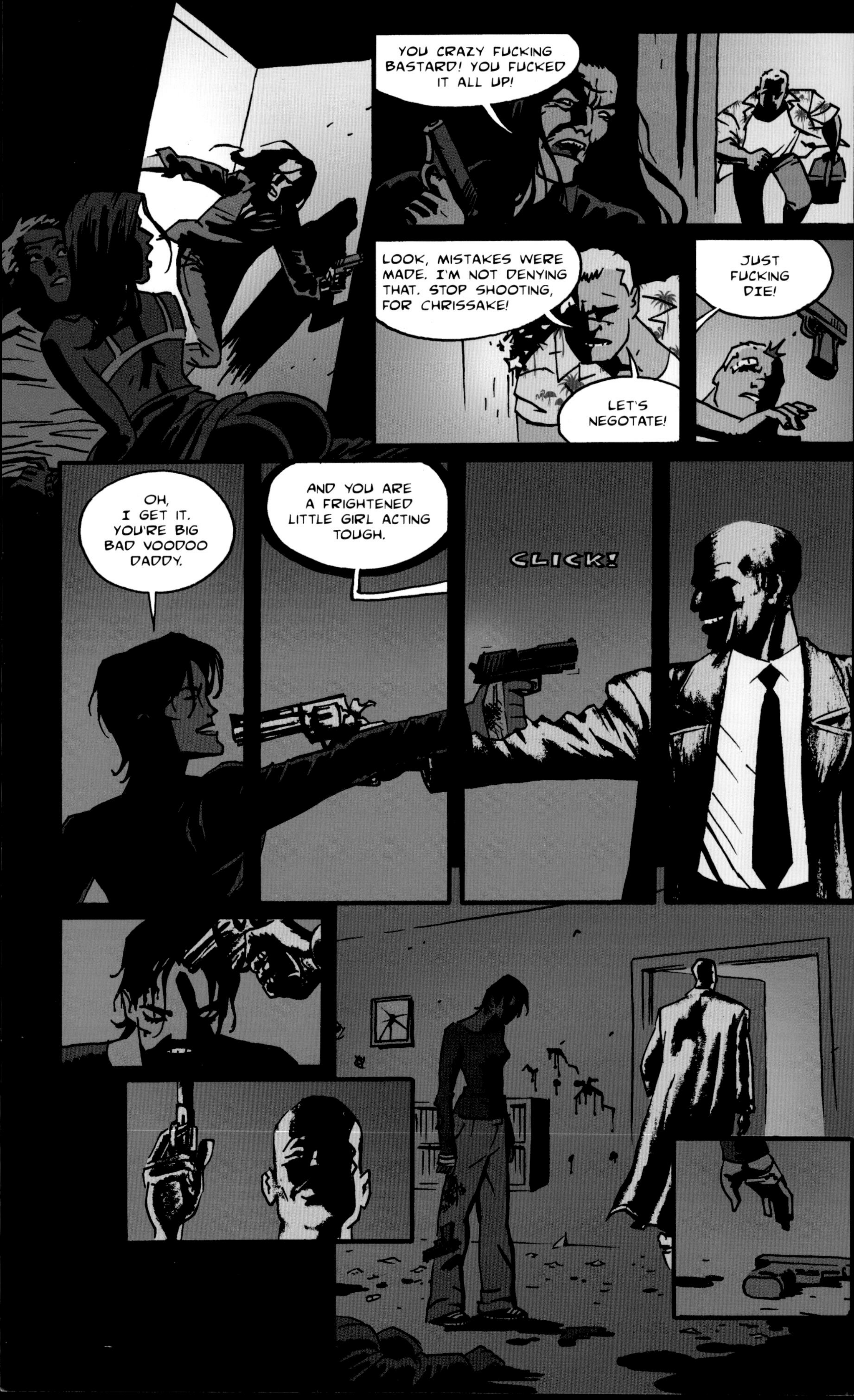
YOU CRAZY FUCKING BASTARD! YOU FUCKED IT ALL UP!
LOOK, MISTAKES WERE MADE. I'M NOT DENYING THAT. STOP SHOOTING, FOR CHRISSAKE!
LET'S NEGOTIATE!
JUST FUCKING DIE!
OH, I GET IT. YOU'RE BIG BAD VOODOO DADDY.
AND YOU ARE A FRIGHTENED LITTLE GIRL ACTING TOUGH.
CLICK!

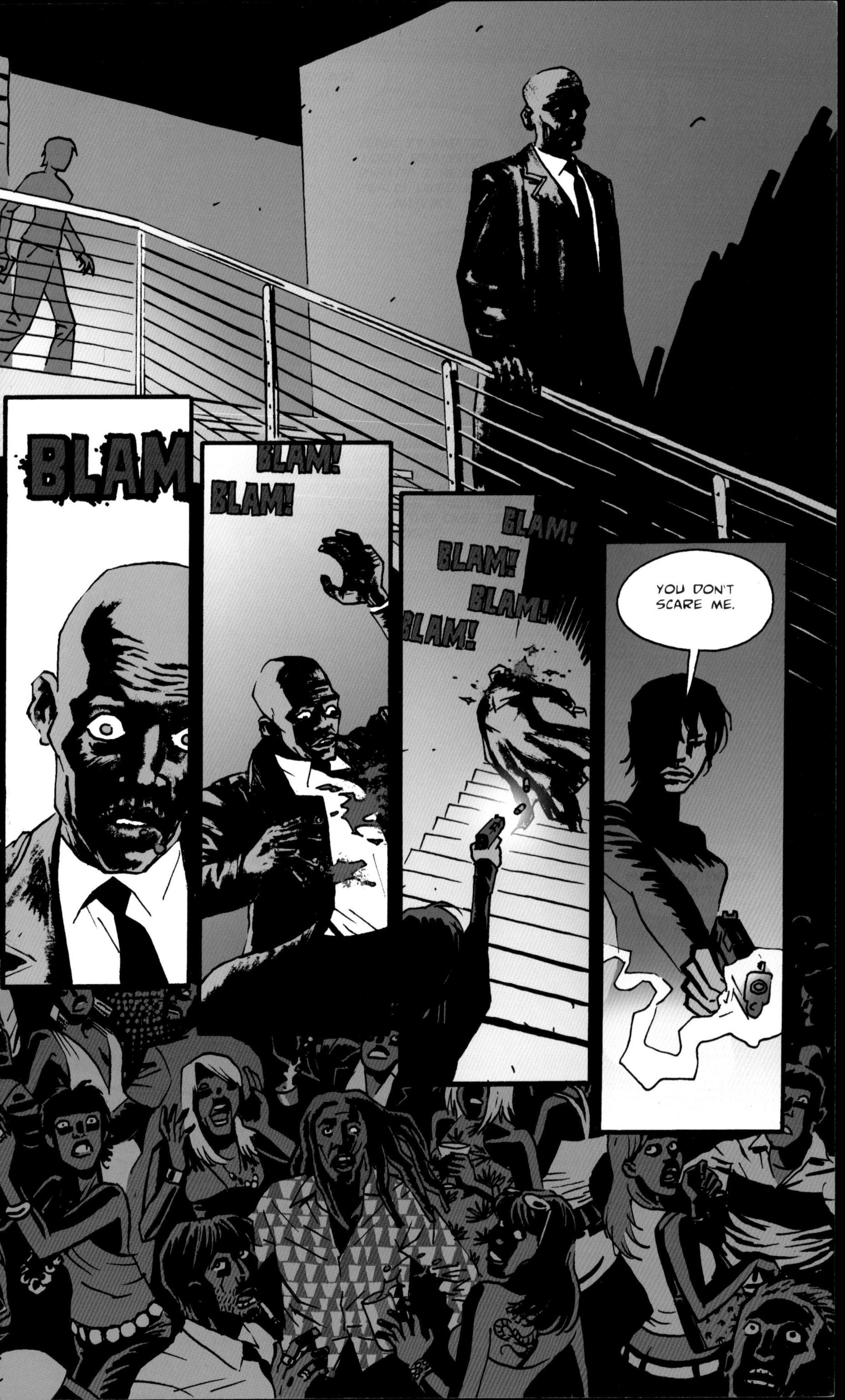
BLAM
BLAM!
BLAM!
BLAM!
BLAM!
BLAM!
BLAM!
YOU DON'T SCARE ME.

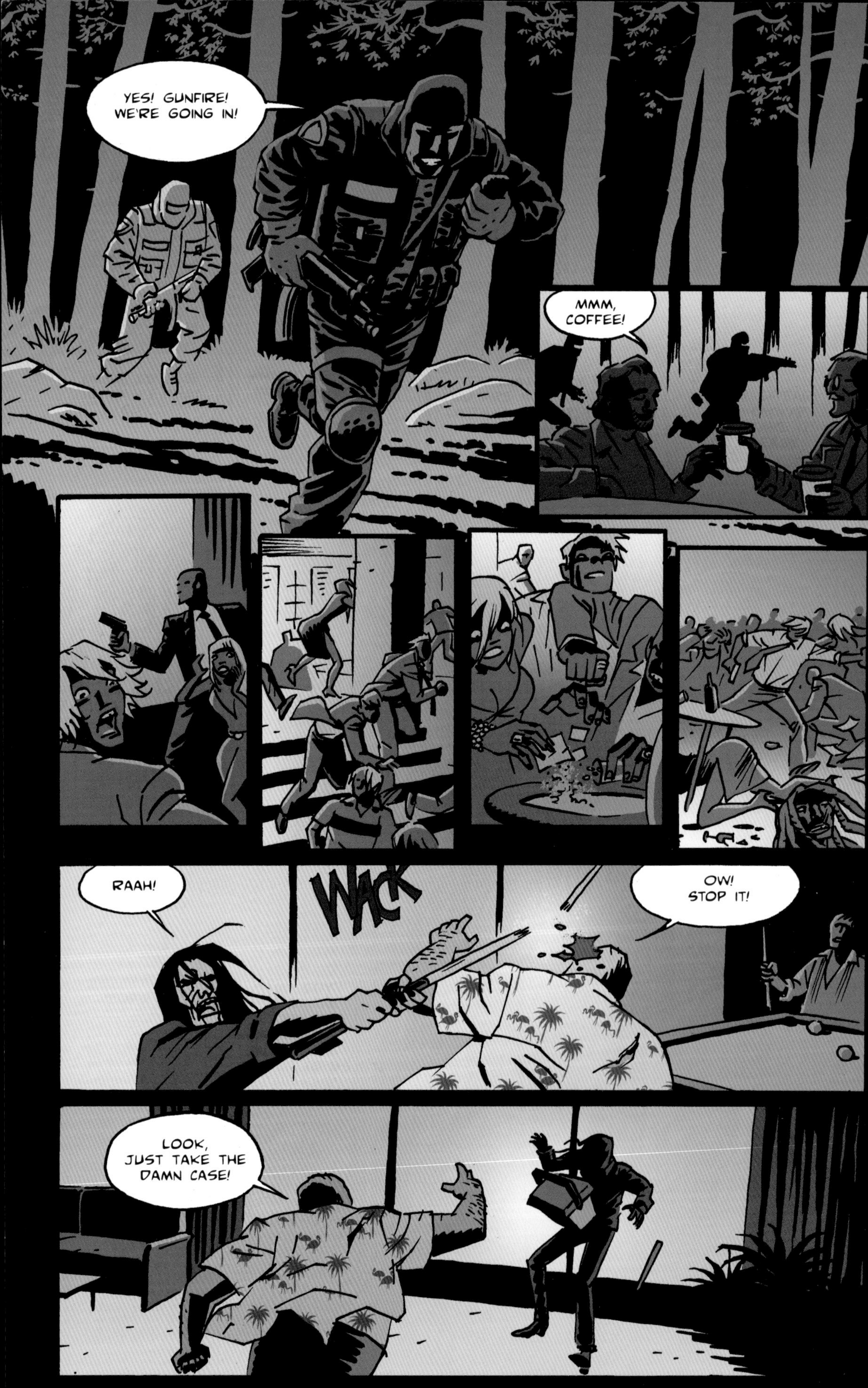
YES! GUNFIRE! WE'RE GOING IN!
MMM, COFFEE!
RAAH!
WACK
OW! STOP IT!
LOOK, JUST TAKE THE DAMN CASE!

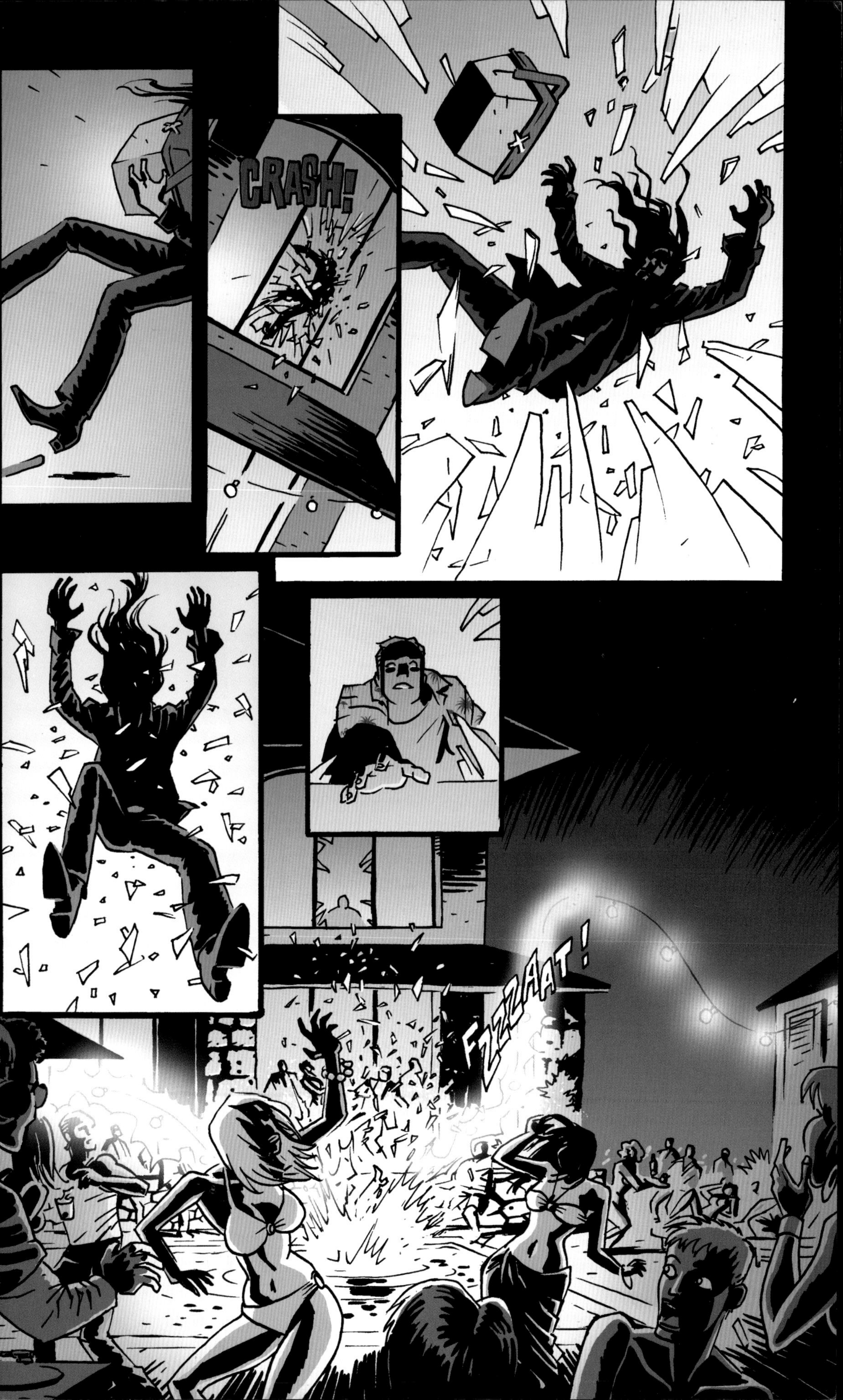
CRASH!
FZZZAAT!

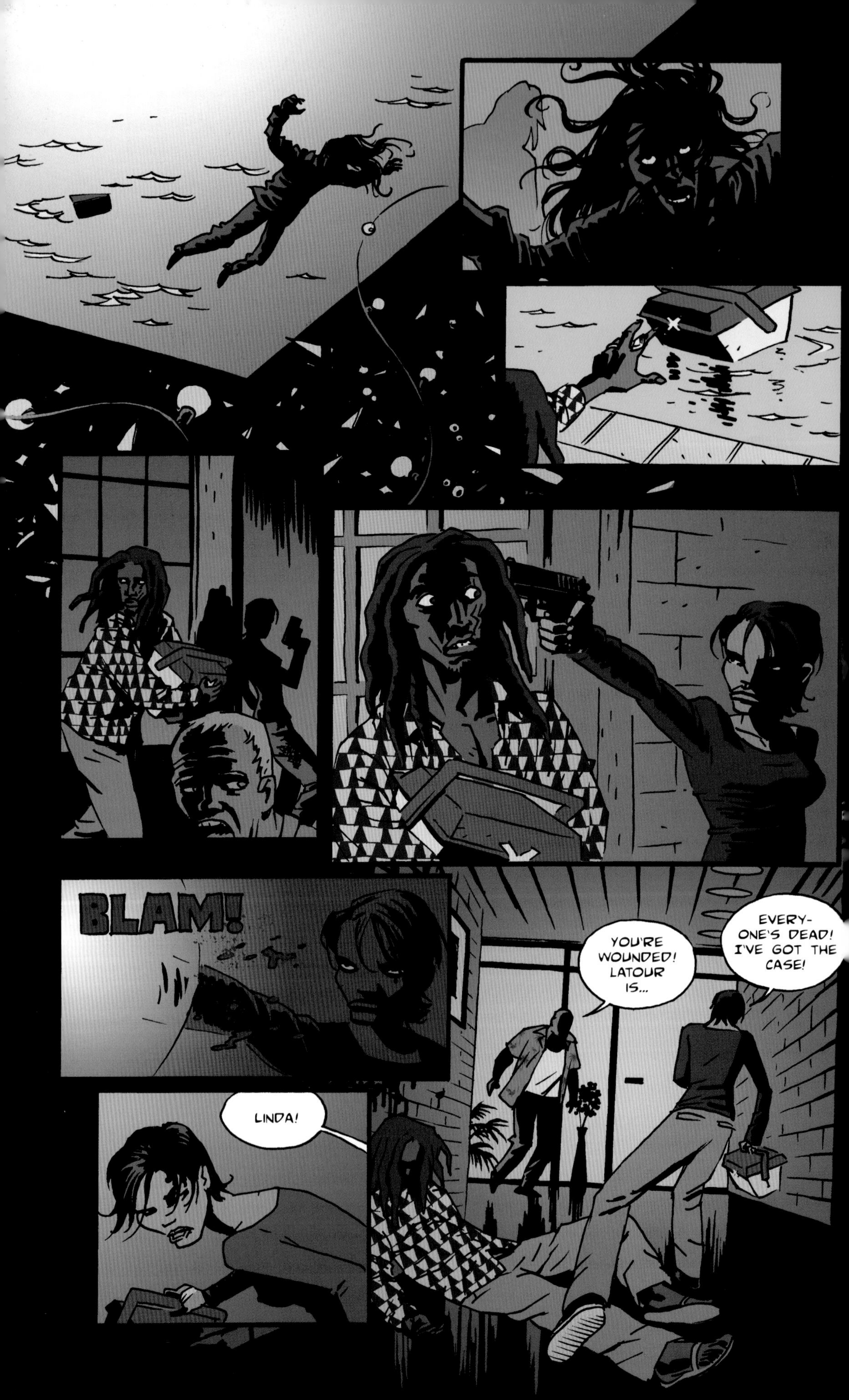
BLAM!
YOU'RE WOUNDED! LATOUR IS...
EVERY-ONE'S DEAD! I'VE GOT THE CASE!
LINDA!

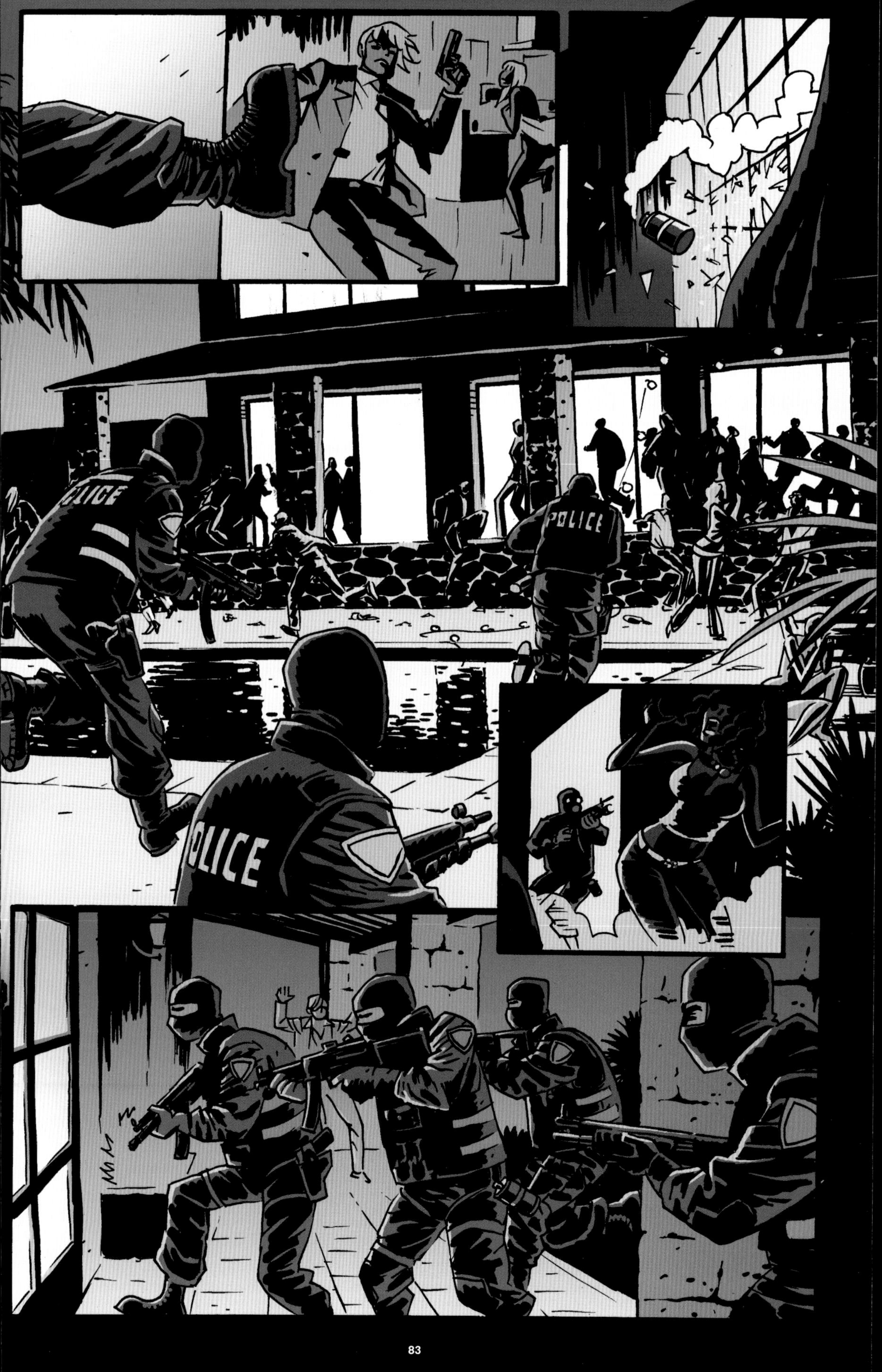

POLICE
OLICE

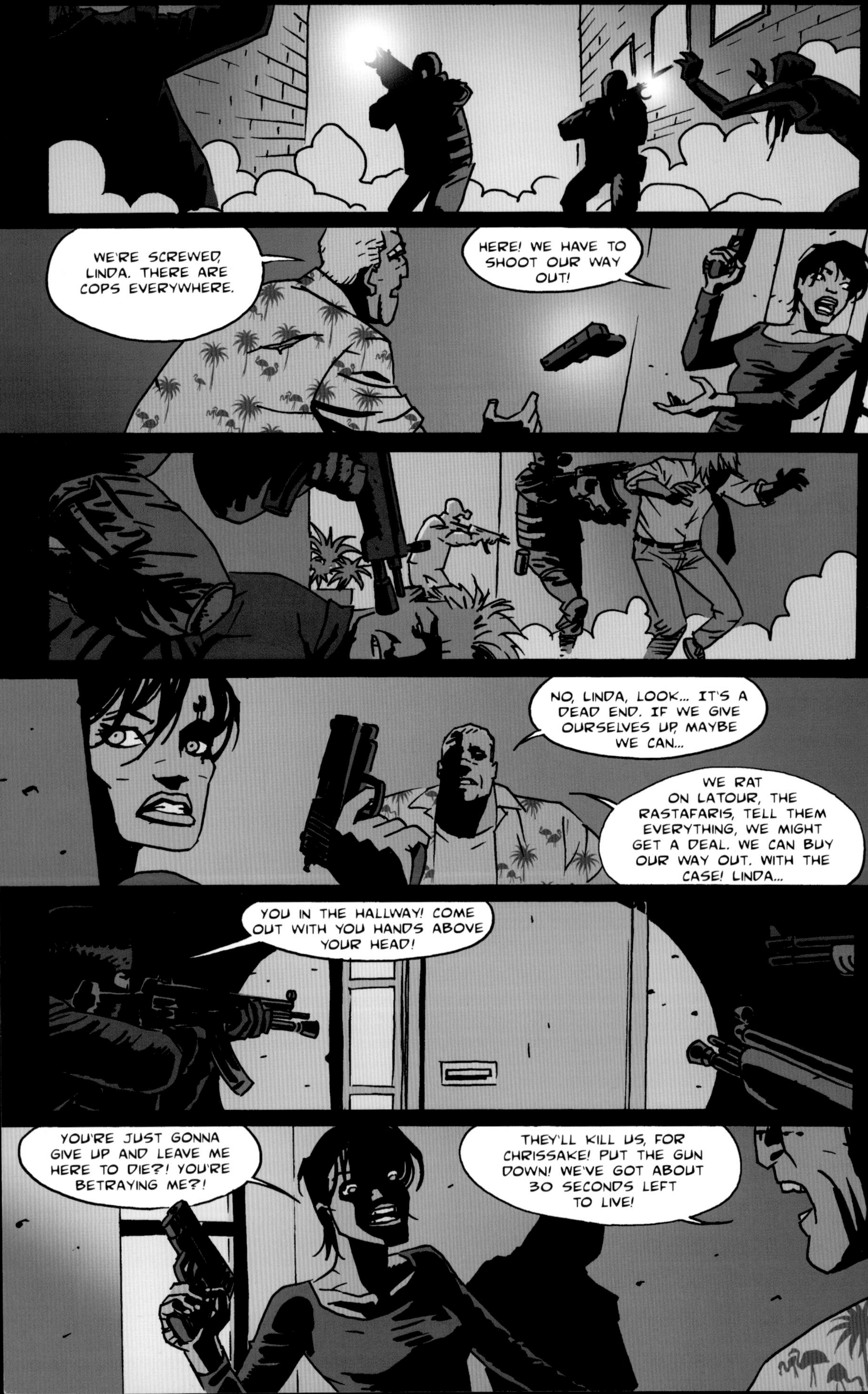
WE'RE SCREWED, LINDA. THERE ARE COPS EVERYWHERE.
HERE! WE HAVE TO SHOOT OUR WAY OUT!
NO, LINDA, LOOK... IT'S A DEAD END. IF WE GIVE OURSELVES UP, MAYBE WE CAN...
WE RAT ON LATOUR, THE RASTAFARIS, TELL THEM EVERYTHING, WE MIGHT GET A DEAL. WE CAN BUY OUR WAY OUT. WITH THE CASE! LINDA...
YOU IN THE HALLWAY! COME OUT WITH YOU HANDS ABOVE YOUR HEAD!
YOU'RE JUST GONNA GIVE UP AND LEAVE ME HERE TO DIE?! YOU'RE BETRAYING ME?!
THEY'LL KILL US, FOR CHRISSAKE! PUT THE GUN DOWN! WE'VE GOT ABOUT 30 SECONDS LEFT TO LIVE!

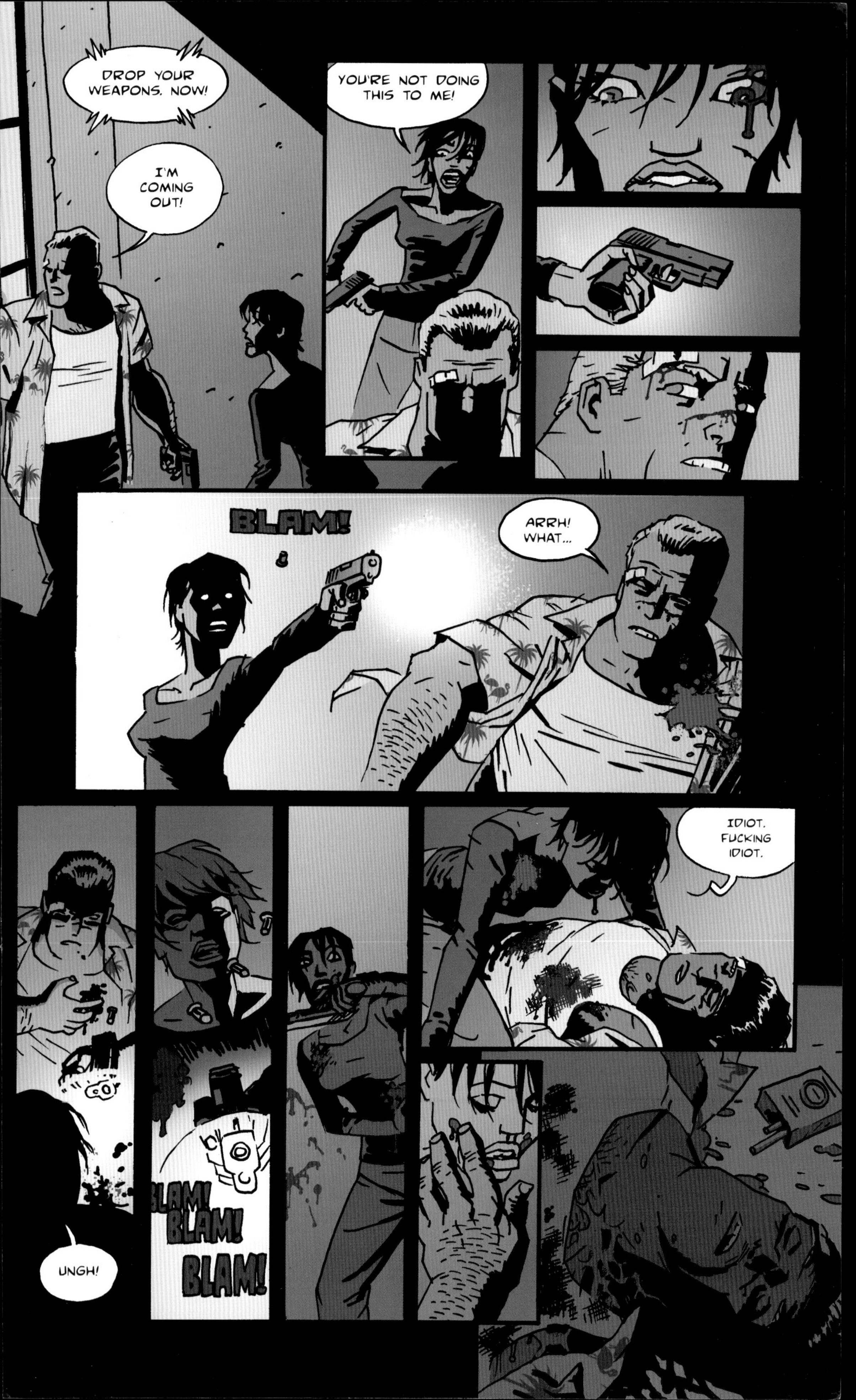
DROP YOUR WEAPONS. NOW!
I'M COMING OUT!
YOU'RE NOT DOING THIS TO ME!
BLAM!
ARRH! WHAT...
UNGH!
BLAM! BLAM! BLAM!
IDIOT. FUCKING IDIOT.

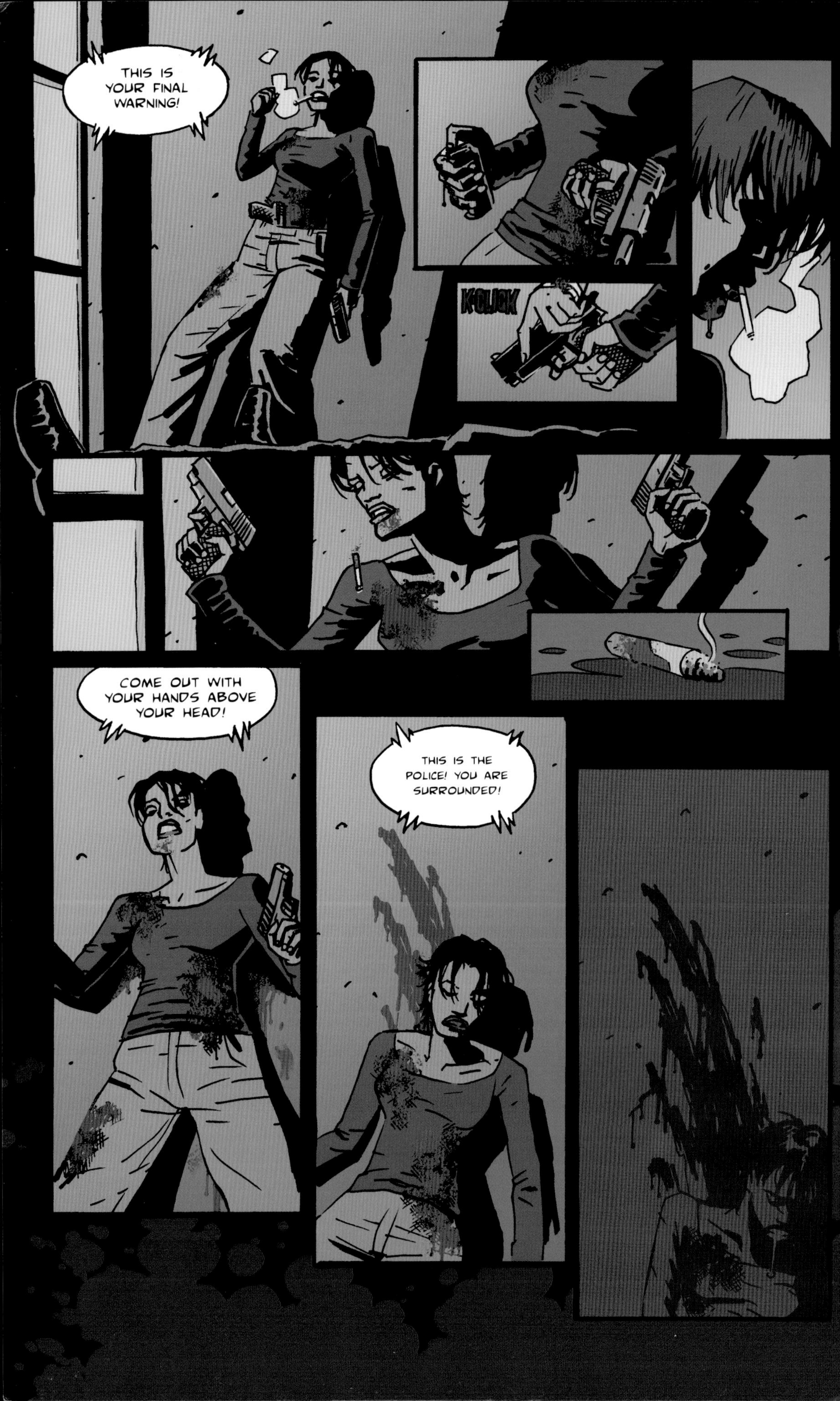
THIS IS YOUR FINAL WARNING!
K-CLICK
COME OUT WITH YOUR HANDS ABOVE YOUR HEAD!
THIS IS THE POLICE! YOU ARE SURROUNDED!

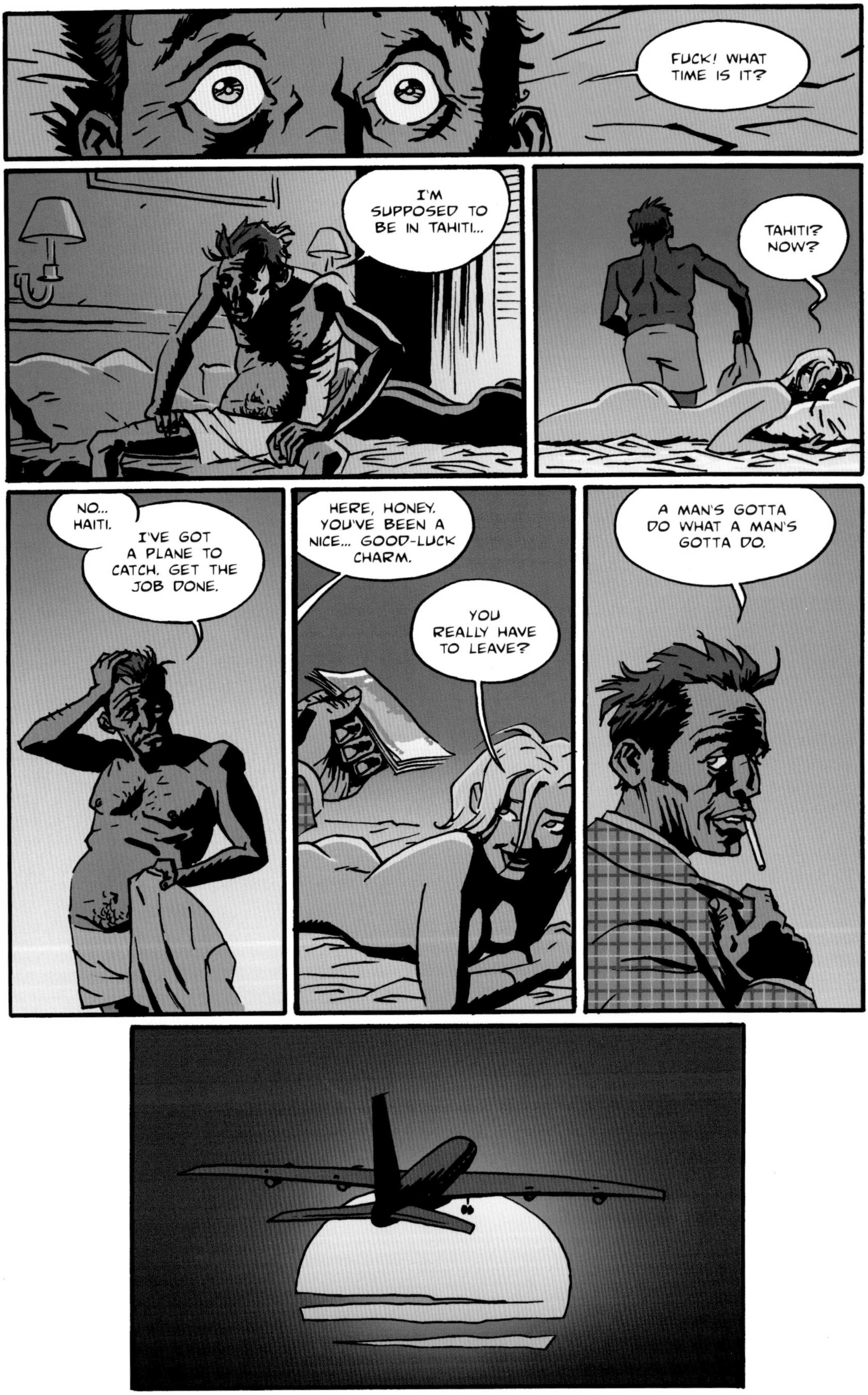
FUCK! WHAT TIME IS IT?
I'M SUPPOSED TO BE IN TAHITI...
TAHITI? NOW?
NO... HAITI.
I'VE GOT A PLANE TO CATCH. GET THE JOB DONE.
HERE, HONEY. YOU'VE BEEN A NICE... GOOD-LUCK CHARM.
YOU REALLY HAVE TO LEAVE?
A MAN'S GOTTA DO WHAT A MAN'S GOTTA DO.

THE END

Afterword

Sometimes it takes a long time to cook up a story.

This one simmered all through the late '90s, as I added ingredients along the way. It all started with the want for a female lead, something about drugs and violence, set in a non-specific European city. Then a friend of mine introduced a title, stolen from a French rap song, and added the spice of the Rastafaris.

Years later, another friend, Olav Junker Kjær, helped pull the whole thing together, as I reused the storyline of an old roleplaying-game scenario of mine. Olav helped control my ideas, structured the plot and made a first attempt of a script, which I later scavenged. I learned a lot from our months of sparring, talking over story, characters, and dialogue, putting our protagonists in seemingly impossible predicaments–and then getting them out of it.

While Olav and I developed the story, I worked the visuals, inspired mostly by Asian action movies and French caper movies of the '60s. I wanted to put EVERYTHING I liked into this stew.

Meanwhile, life got in the way. Illustration work, mostly, pretending to be a dedicated student at English and Film studies at the University, later hiding my comics under perspective drawings at the School of Architecture as the teachers walked by on a rare occasion. I finally skipped school altogether, and started working freelance out of the renowned Gimle studios in Copenhagen, setting up my workspace next to Peter Snejbjerg, a long-time comic book artist working on titles such as *The Books of Magic, Starman, The Light Brigade, and A God Somewhere.* Watching, learning. Sometimes doing pencils and layouts for Peter–uncredited but paid work. I put out a couple of graphic novels in Denmark in my own name, several roleplaying-game books. I got a girlfriend and a baby girl.

Continued...

All the while the *Concubine* brewed.

In 2008 it finally came out on the Danish market. My huge ambitions and insecurities as a storyteller had finally given way to a pragmatic get-the-job-done attitude, gained from years of illustration and storyboard work, and the limited working hours gained from becoming a parent. *The Devil's Concubine* was finished in between stroller walks and diaper changes. My then 1-year-old daughter once flicked through a black-and-white print out of the book, pointed at someone getting shot in the knees, and said "Ow, ow." Smart kid. Don't do this at home.

Hope you enjoy reading this book as much as I did making it, returning to sniff the pot with the same enthusiasm all through these years. It was always meant for the American market, so this is an absolute thrill for me. I have been entertained by American movies, comics, and books all my life. Thanks for letting me entertain you back.

My next book will be served a lot quicker. That's a promise.

Palle Schmidt
Copenhagen
July 2010

Palle Schmidt is a Danish illustrator and writer. After a stint in roleplaying games, he now focuses his energy on graphic novels, crime novels, and movie scripts besides doing illustration work for children's books, storyboards, and rapid vizualizing at corporate events and workshops. He lives in Copenhagen with his wife and two daughters.

SKETCHBOOK

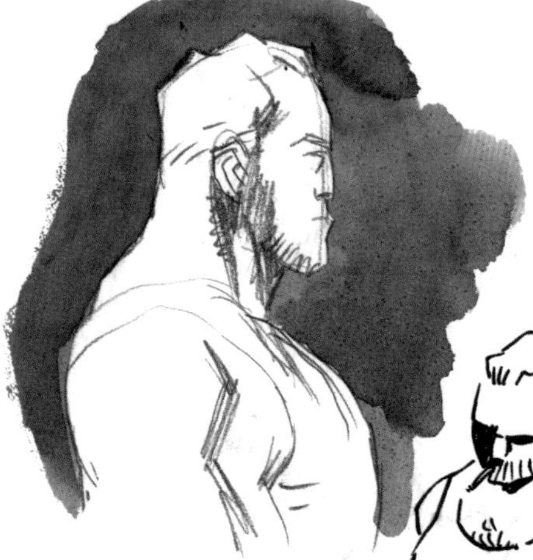

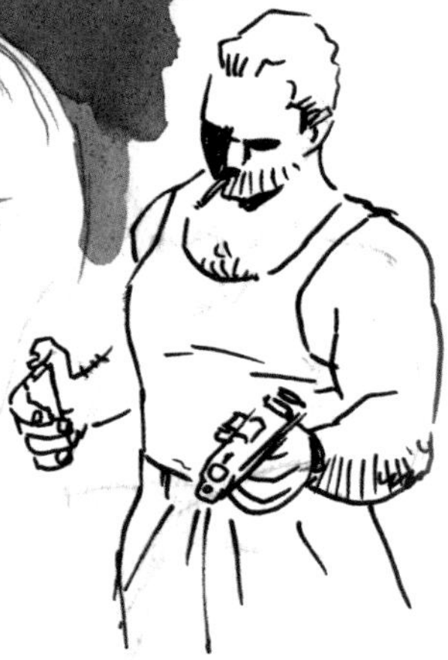

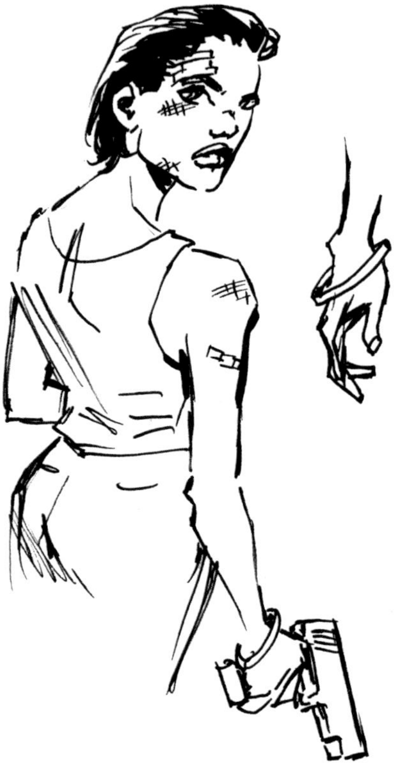

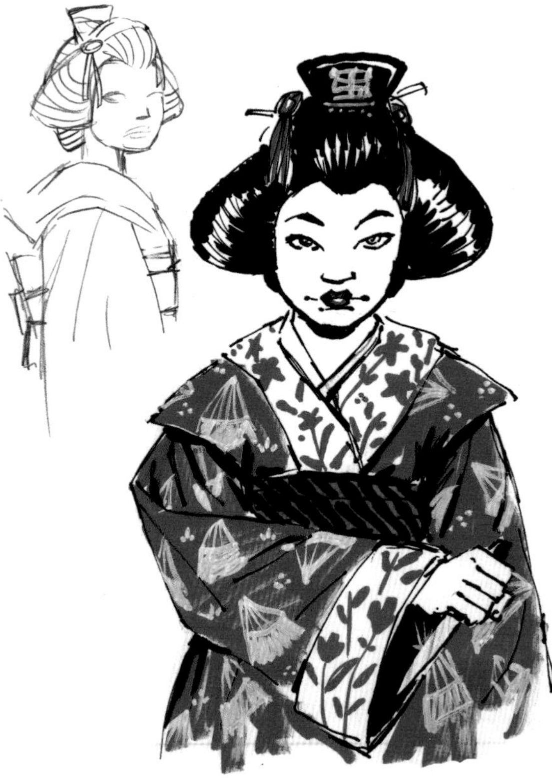

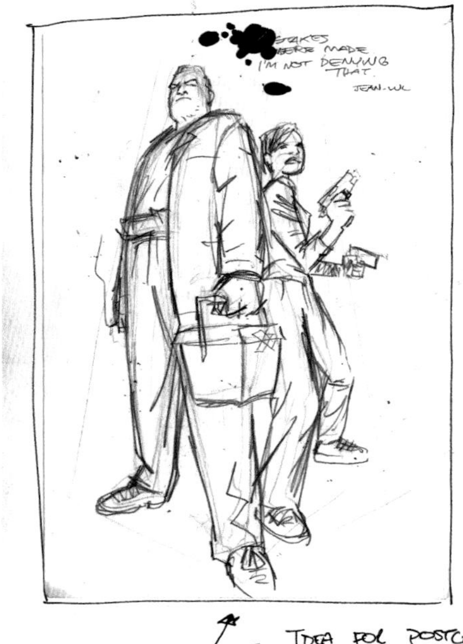
MADE
I'M NOT DENYING
THAT.

IDEA FOR POSTCA
SERIES

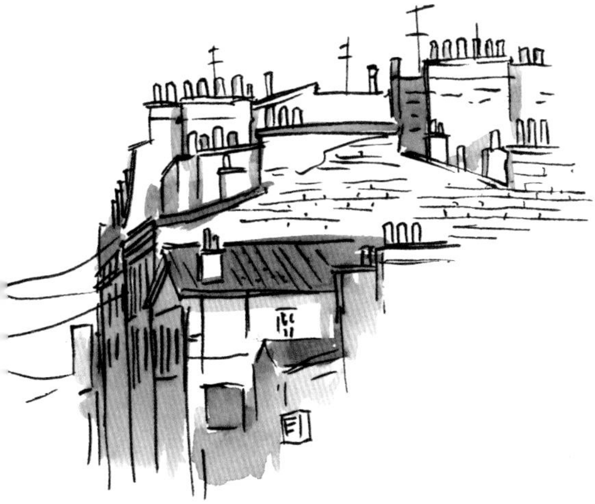

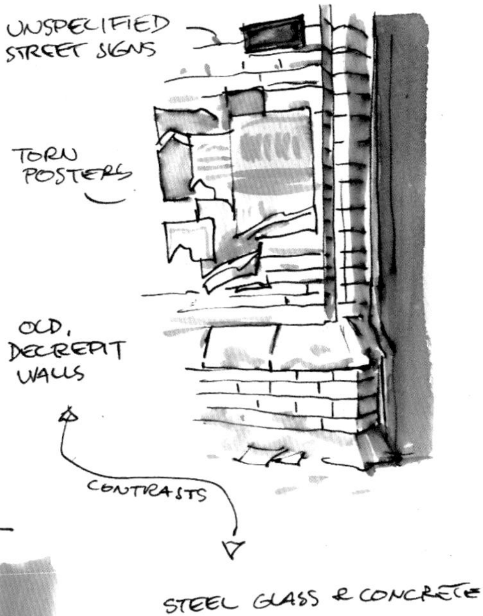
UNSPECIFIED STREET SIGNS
TORN POSTERS
OLD, DECREPIT WALLS
CONTRASTS
STEEL GLASS & CONCRETE

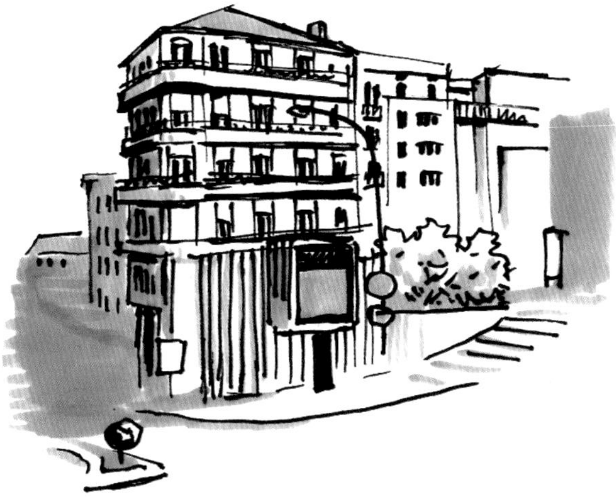

ELEMENTS OF FRANCE, GERMANY, SPAIN

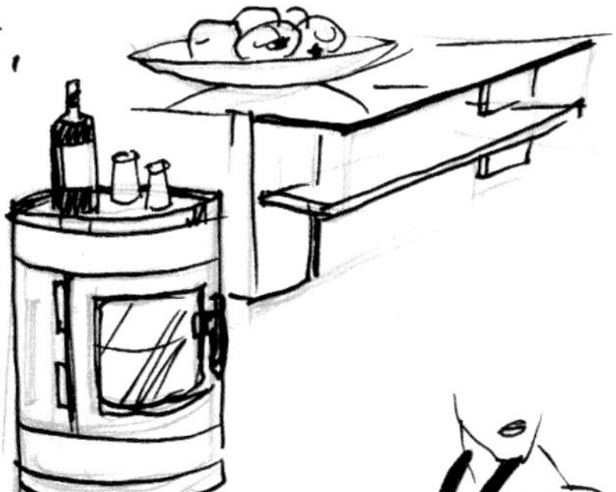

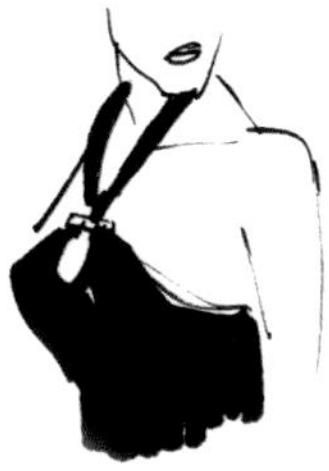

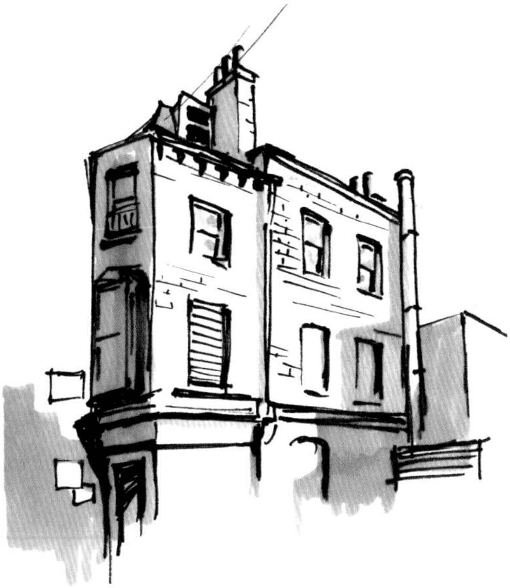

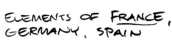

MODERN WEAPONS, REFERENCES (MUSIC ETC.)

60's PATTERNS, COLORS, CLOTHING, FURNITURE, ARCHITECTURE

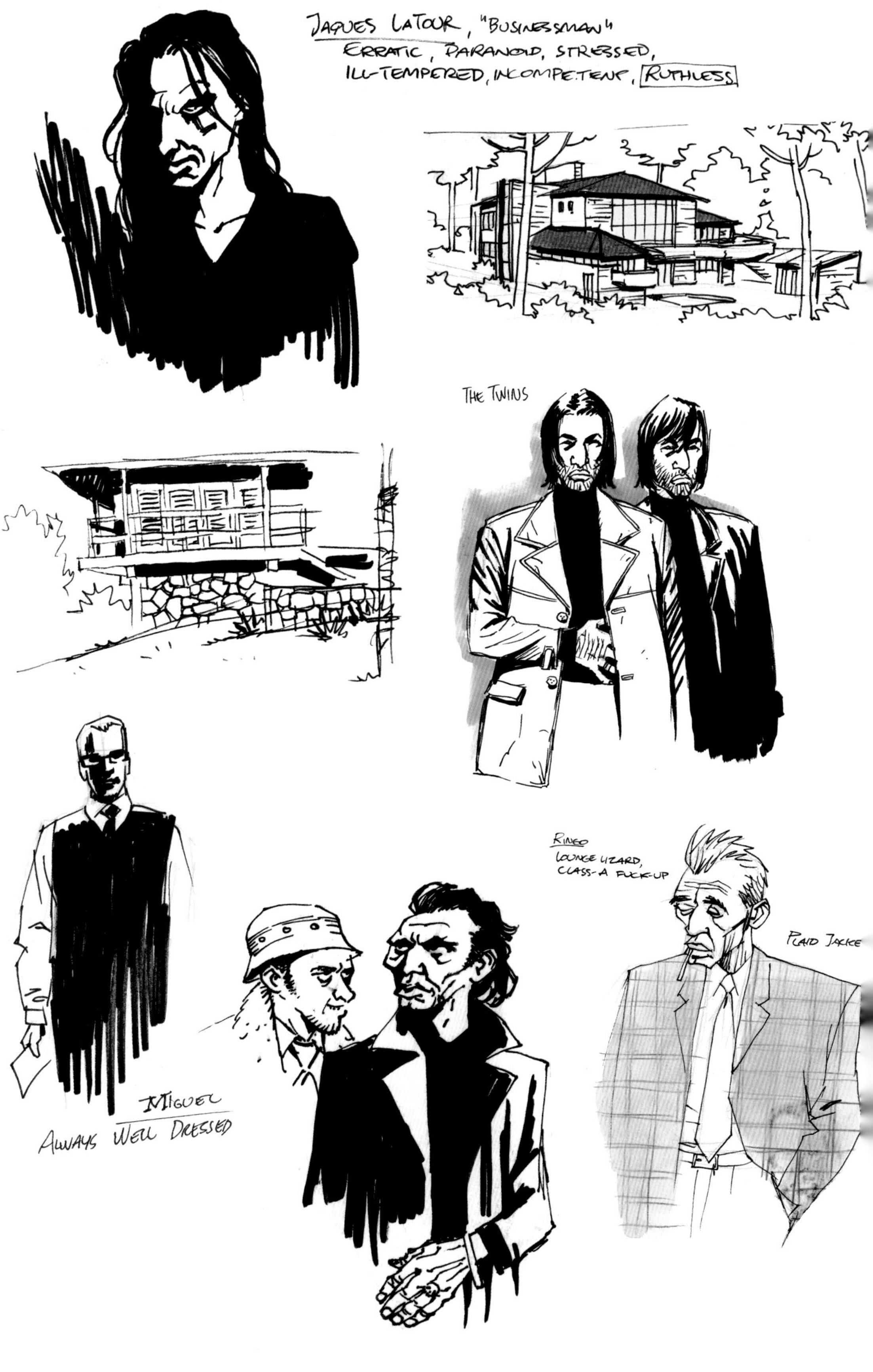
JAQUES LATOUR, "BUSINESSMAN"
ERRATIC, PARANOID, STRESSED,
ILL-TEMPERED, INCOMPETENT, RUTHLESS
THE TWINS
RINGO
LOUNGE LIZARD,
CLASS-A FUCK-UP
PLAID JACKE
MIGUEL
ALWAYS WELL DRESSED

BALD, BONY
FEATURES

NOTE:
THE HAITIAN IS
IN BLACK & WHITE!

ALPHONSE

MAYNARD

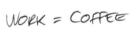

WORK = COFFEE

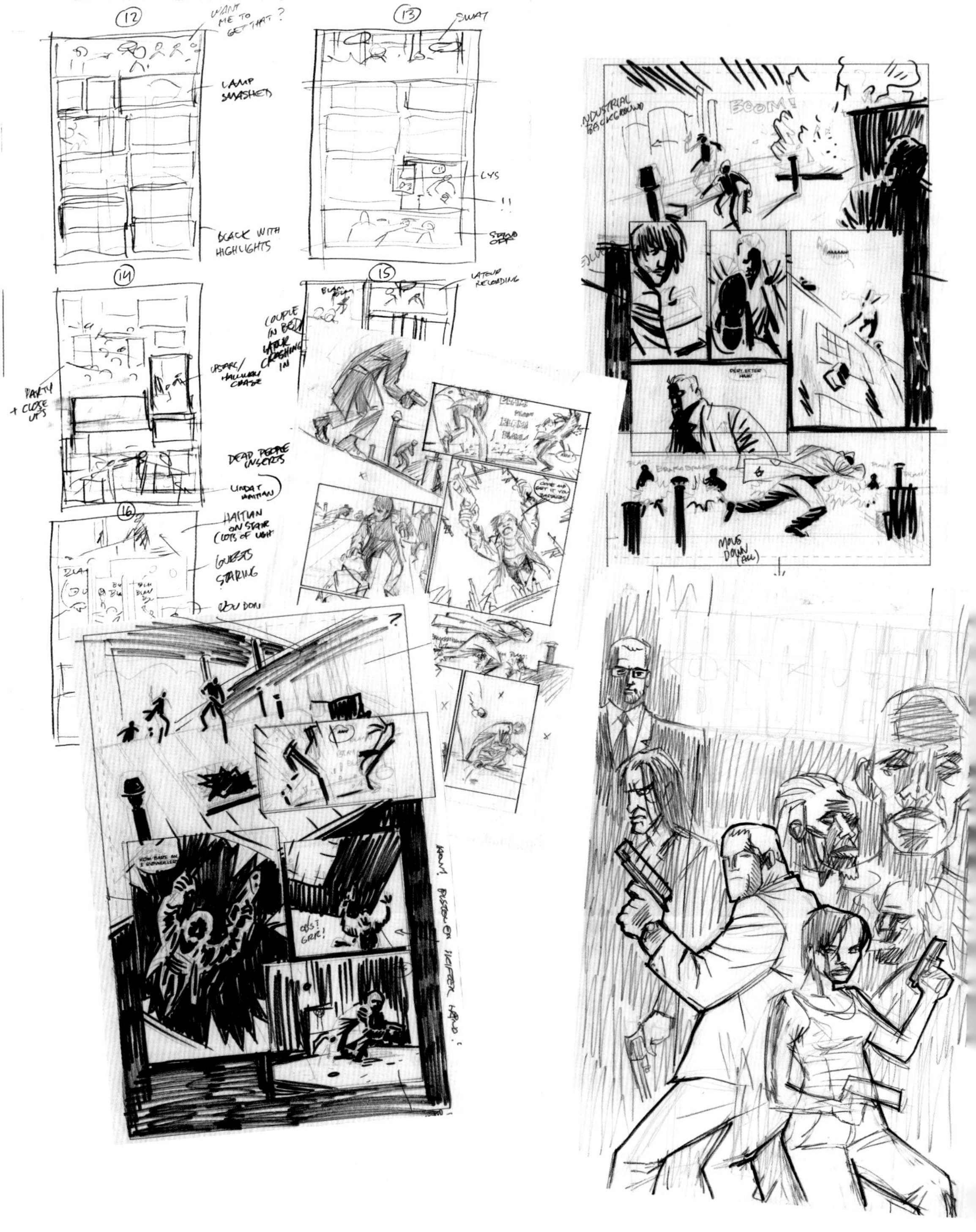

12
WANT ME TO GET THAT?
LAMP SMASHED
BLACK WITH HIGHLIGHTS
13
SWAT
LYS
!!
14
PARTY + CLOSE UPS
STAIRS/HALLWAY CHASE
DEAD PEOPLE INSERTS
15
COUPLE IN BED LATER CRASHING IN
16
GUESTS STARING
BOOM!

For more on the making of this book, visit
www. D E V I L S C O N C U B I N E .com